Sincerely,

E. S. Simmons.

A SOLUTION

OF THE

RACE PROBLEM IN THE SOUTH.

(AN ESSAY.)

BY

ENOCH SPENCER SIMMONS,
OF THE NORTH CAROLINA BAR.

RALEIGH, N. C.
Presses of Edwards & Broughton.
1898.

DEDICATED

MEMORY OF MY MOTHER.

PREFACE.

The author of this work has been in no way prompted to write it by any feeling or disposition to do the negro any injustice, but by a desire to deal with the greatest problem that has ever confronted our Southland in any period of its history, and one which deeply concerns all the people of our Union—to deal with the facts as they are now presenting themselves to thoughtful minds, and to suggest a plan which, if adopted, will be a solution of the most perplexing and intricate problem.

This problem has agitated the minds of the foremost thinkers of the South since Lee's surrender at Appomattox. Earnest men—men desirous of being eminently just to both races—have given time and study to this question. Those who have given to the public their thoughts and the result of their labors have as yet mainly advised the people of the North to be patient while we in the South, in our own way, set ourselves to the task of settling these constantly arising new phases of the problem, insisting the while that these new matters would adjust themselves; and so the South hoped that time would find the races in harmonious union, living in brotherly love and peaceful communion, resulting in the glorious upbuilding and development of our country, than which none has ever been more blessed with nature's gifts. But alas! hope is deferred, and the heart of the South is made sick. Thoughtful men see in the distant sky the mere speck of a cloud, which, by the best brain of our land, has been carefully examined and found to be unmistakably the nucleus around which is gathering, as time rolls on, those volcanic dangers which will explode and pour upon future posterity its all-destructive lava.

To avert the awful consequences to future generations is the task which, in this work, has engaged the mind and labor of the author.

One has said "Disappointment sinks the heart of man, but the renewal of hope brings consolation." With renewed energy we set ourselves at this task in the hope of enlisting the efforts of wise statesmen, brave men, earnest men and just men, who, for the sake of unborn posterity, for their love of the people of the South, of both races, will undertake to further the work of the crude suggestions contained in these pages. If the author has succeeded in engaging the thoughtful attention of wise men of this country, who in turn will take up the work and carry it on to completion, then certainly he will feel amply repaid for his pains, knowing that at least he has played a small part in removing the one cause, above all others, which stands in the very gateway of the progress and prosperity of the South and the happiness of future generations.

Sincerely,   E. S. SIMMONS.

WASHINGTON, N. C., *October 19, 1897.*

CONTENTS.

CHAPTER VIII.

CHAPTER IX.

CHAPTER X.

CHAPTER XI.

CHAPTER XII.

CHAPTER XIII.

CHAPTER XIV.

CHAPTER XV.

THE RACE PROBLEM.

CHAPTER I

THE SOLUTION OF THE PROBLEM.

More than sixty-five years ago, Bishop Bascom, as unmistakably appears from his writings, foreshadowed the race troubles we now have in the South. While not in language direct, inferentially, his words disclose the fact that he then saw in the signs of the times, the certain evidence of freedom to come to the enslaved negroes within the United States. With these convictions he sought to avert the dangers of the two races inhabiting the same soil in years to come by colonizing the free-born negroes of the United States in Liberia.

Mrs. Harriet Beecher Stowe, in "Uncle Tom's Cabin," makes George Harris, in his letter to a friend, talk of Liberia as the haven of refuge and settlement of the negroes in the United States. From which Republic, colonization and christianity would be disseminated throughout all Africa; again, this benighted continent would be elevated to the position of glory, fame and distinction, enjoyed by them in the remote ages of antiquity.

Bishop Atticus G. Haygood, of the Southern Methodist Church, in his " Brother in Black," offered as a solution of the race problem in the South, Christian forbearance, brotherly love, patient tolerance, better and higher education of the negro, morally, mentally and physically.

Henry W. Grady, in whose early death the South sustained a great loss, plead with the North to let us alone, while we of the South would adjust race differences, as each new phase of the problem would arise. Many other lesser lights have contributed to the magazines of our country their views, the trend of all which was to plead for patience and forbearance of the North, while we in the South worked out the plan of our own salvation.

One great truth can be gathered from all these, to-wit: The fact that the presence of the negro in the South would bring and has brought upon us troubles of mountainous proportions, which, indeed, threatens the peace, happiness and prosperity, yes, the very life of our Southern country.

A careful examination of the present condition of the South unfolds to the enquirer the lamentable fact, that however well meant the claim of latter day philosophers, are not sustained by events actually transpiring throughout the South, and the unmistakable evidence of facts, proving greater race divergence, and that the gulf between the two widens, deepens and lengthens, with every revolution of the great wheel of time.

Bishop Bascom and Mrs. Harriet Beecher Stowe's plan was at the time they wrote undoubtedly right, as the means to be employed in averting race troubles in this country, yet it would not be practicable at this time. The negro is a citizen of the United States, and as such we have no right to deport him.

All thoughtful persons no longer doubt the necessity of solving our race troubles. No thoughtful person, with a regard for the truth, will deny the presence and existence of such, and instead of lessening they are daily, hourly and constantly increasing in dangerous proportions. We would solve the problem of our race troubles in the South by separating the two races and colonizing the negro in the southern part of the United States. We insist, no other solution of the problem can be given. To expect the two races so materially differing from each other, as does the Negro and the Caucasian, to live together on the same soil in peace and harmony, would be in violation of all natural laws, and, therefore, impossible.

Assuming that colonization is the only solution of the problem, we will in the pages of this work undertake to prove its practicability and the absolute necessity for it, and the great dangers sure to come to posterity, if neglected.

CHAPTER II.

" RACE FEELING IN THE SOUTH."

However much well meaning people in the South may wish it otherwise, it nevertheless is true. that the feeling of dislike between the two races is becoming intensified as time wears on. The chasm is deepening and widening into a more impassible gulf each year. This fact is much deplored by many of both races, and while both regret it, yet it is true. and cannot be helped.

The author here desires to say for himself, he has always entertained a kindly feeling for the colored race of people. That among them there are those for whom he has the most sincere and affectionate regard. An old colored woman, now living at Pantego, N. C.. more than eighty-five years of age, always known in my father's family as "Aunt Hester." remarkable in many ways, chief among them. she has had born to her twenty-six children. Trusty. faithful and true. devoted to the memory of my mother and father. always speaking of them as tenderly and affectionately as if they had been of her own flesh and blood. It is not often we see the old woman: it affords us as much pleasure to have her visit us as if she was one of our own family.

The other old favorites of my father's family have long since passed away, among them my nurse; we have a tender and affectionate regard for their memories, and like their children. Only recently we had a letter from Prince, a boy of my own age. We have not seen each other nor heard from each other since we parted on the plantation, after Lee's surrender. Indeed, he writes, he did not know where we were. In this we were alike; we had not heard from him. Among other things, he says: " The last time I saw you was in Hyde County. I thought the world of you. One thing you did was to take up for me if I got in a quarrel. I have heard recently from a white friend, who knows all about you of late years; and it makes my poor heart leap with joy to hear from my young master. I suppose my old Massa and Missus are dead and gone long ago. May God bless them. I hope you will at least think enough of me to write and tell me all about them in their latter days, as I often think of how much service I might have been to them. Give my regards to your brother and sister and all the family—you I remember best of all."

Of course we answered the letter. We were, indeed, glad to hear from Prince. Many were the happy days we spent in childhood together. Notwithstanding my own kind feeling for this race, it is plain to any thoughtful mind obser-

vant of events, constantly occurring, however
much we might wish it otherwise, the races
have for some time past reached a point of divergence in feeling of dislike for each other,
which widens in extent, as the lines of time are
further drawn.   If Dr. Haygood, author of that
praiseworthy work, "Our Brother in Black,"
and others, who wrote fifteen or more years ago,
could carefully investigate conditions of to-day,
they would reach a far different conclusion, see-
ing the necessity, not so much for the immediate present, but for posterity, of the separation
of the two races.

There are causes for this growing dislike.   It
is the purpose of this chapter to deal with a few.
After the smoke of battle had cleared away and
the Southern soldier had returned to his home,
wasted and in many instances destroyed by the
ravages of war, with farms grown up, fences
gone, ditches filled, the picture of desolation and
dispair seen everywhere—finding himself and
his neighbors poor indeed—like brave men set
themselves to work to repair their lost fortunes.
No people ever tried harder to adjust themselves
to new condition.   Slavery and its incidents,
the institutions of a century, abolished; and in
its place the slaves made free, with the right of
ballot given them, accompanied with all the evil
consequences, attending the habiliment of this
ignorant race of people, with the rights of citi-

zenship, were conditions to be met and dealt with
by our Southern people. How well they did it,
the future historian will tell.

This race of people, so lately slave property,
had been made citizens with all the rights of
such, as we have seen, under the Constitution
of this Union. Our people, knowing that the
best results for government and society flow
from the minds and hearts of a people prepared
by education to appreciate the necessities of civilization and good government, set themselves to
work, both with mind and heart, to prepare this
race for a proper appreciation of their newly-
made duties of citizenship and its responsibilities. With generous hand taxes were gathered,
our Constitutions re-written, distributing the tax
revenues for public school purposes equally between the two races in proportion to number,
school houses built, schools taught; all this done,
too, with taxes raised upon the property of the
white people, except the small parts raised upon
the poll, for the negro then had no property, and
but little now. To say that our Southern people did this grudgingly, as some are wont to do,
would not be in any degree borne out by the
facts; rather, the people of the South, both with
mind and heart, wish to give their old slaves and
children a fair chance in the race of life; they
were not forgetful of the fidelity with which he
stood guard, protecting our mothers and sisters,

wives and children at home, while his master
was upon the battle field, fighting to perpetuate
the institution of his slavery; the happy memories of plantation life, baby and childhood, with
the lullabys of black mammies, the cabin with
banjo and songs of Uncle Tom, the development
of our Southland in other days by the use of his
strong arm, lingered in the minds of our people.

Whatever may be said to the contrary, it was
true, indeed, as many of the old slaves will testify, that their masters had a kindly regard for
them and wished them to do well. The younger
generation, children of slave owning parents, including many young men who wore the gray at
the close of the war, had been tenderly nursed
by black mammies, who love their nurslings
with the devotion of mothers; then, too, there
were many " Uncle Toms," who watched the
interest and affairs of their masters with a devotion and fidelity never surpassed. The pride of
their lives was the success of their master's children.

These sentiments, and sincere regard for black
mammies and Uncle Toms, caused our law-
makers, who were principally ex-slave holders
or the children of such, without stint, not grudgingly, but generously, earnestly desiring their
success and the success of their descendants, to
do all in their power to make provisions for the
education and happiness of this race. After we

had become accustomed to these new conditions, for a time, things went well, the leavening influence of black mammy and Uncle Tom did much for the good of their race, these old ones tenderly regarded by their old masters and the younger generation whom they had nursed and helped to raise, stood a barrier, a rock of safety, between the heat and passion of the younger ones that were fast coming up. The writer wants to say with sincerity that the old slaves made good citizens; most of them, indeed, well nigh all, have passed into the shades of forgetfulness. The wisdom of their advice, we regret to say, is no longer cherished in the memories of their descendants. A generation has come and another gone since the beginning of these conditions, and instead of a realization of our cherished hopes, disappointment is seen everywhere. Thirty-two years of generous education has for its reward in this race a growing dislike for the people that gave it. Education seems only to have educated well in teaching the recipients of this bounty, better ways of disliking, cheating and defrauding its giver.

Of the generation of negroes now coming on it may be said, truly, their best thoughts, purpose and action are bestowed upon ways to get the white race within their grasp and control. A foolish idea, it is true—one in which their dream of hope will be only a dream, but true withal. Of course those of the white race disposed to help them are discouraged: despair has taken the place of hope; while the thousands who have never entertained any feeling but dislike for this race are made to dislike the negro more because of his ingratitude for the good which has been done him.

You hear it on every side that the white people of the South, owning the property and paying the taxes, have tired of educating this propertyless race, who, in turn for thanks and gratitude, give them all the dislike and animosity common to their nature. There is, no doubt, the sentiment of opposition to the education of the negro by the white man is growing; there is no doubt the negro is responsible for this sentiment. For the generosity of his white friends he has given them, whenever and wherever the opportunity presented, with but few exceptions, bad government, by imposing upon us characterless white men of the baser sort, whose chief ambition, pride and pleasure is to so administer the affairs of government as to disgrace society, insult the honor and dignity of our commonwealth and degrade the patriotic people of the South, who themselves and their ancestry can boast of noble citizenship, and whose only wish and desire is for the prosperity, success and upbuilding of our beautiful Southland, the peace and happiness of our Union.

Is it surprising, then, that the chasm is widening? Oh, but it may be said that the negro is not wholly responsible for this condition of feeling; that bad and contriving white men, with minds indifferent to consequences, incite him to this feeling of dislike, for the purpose of their own self-aggrandizement. This is true, but it adds force and emphasis to the argument. Yes, it is too true, in a land where live brave men and beautiful women, a land where nature has so blended its many gifts, that it can be truly said, There is none other like it to be found anywhere on the globe. A land of magnificent farms and forest trees, of beautiful rivers and picturesque mountains, of broad lakes and sounds, the land of vines and roses, where from nature's conservatory may be cut at all seasons, the richest and rarest flowers; a land which, in truth, flows with milk and honey; a land wherein should live a people than whom none ought to be happier, there is to be found white men, and many of them base white men, men with minds disposed by nature to vicious and desperate ends; men to whom virtue and character are strangers; men fit associates for criminals—so lost to shame and all that is ennobling and elevating that they are willing to arouse and incite the negro race to hatred and dislike of the people of the South, who would be disposed to aid and assist them.

This should not be true. The negro has had a
generation of advantages, educated into a knowledge of better things; but the seed of these bad
and wicked men is sown into a willing and fertile soil. The negro listens and nurtures these
teachings with as much pleasure as his emo-
tional nature permits him to enjoy the teachings
of his favorite minister. So vast is this prejudice and bad feeling between the races growing
that, in those sections wherein the negroes are
in the majority, he becomes intolerably insolent,
impudent and unbearable. He seems to be fully
possessed with the idea that freedom to the negro is not understood by our white people, un-
less he is insulting and insolent. His disposition
is to drive out the white people in those settlements wherein he is largely in the majority by
making it well nigh dangerous for law-abiding
whites to live near by. In this there is hope for
the purpose of this work—it argues that the negro takes kindly to the idea of colonization,
evincing a desire to be left alone.

It is bad faith in the negro who, while conditions existing in the South will not permit him
to fill office, is willing, in order to satisfy his
pique, to elevate men unfit for the discharge of
the duties of office, in part, as a means of punishing their white friends, while they, themselves, are likewise punished, thus showing the
deliberation of his dislike and hatred of the other

race, while at the same time losing sight of the
fact, he is planning for his own ultimate ruin.

Another growing cause of dislike of the white
man by the negro is the want of virtue among
their race—their young women become an easy
prey to the siren voice of passion's tongue. This
incites the jealousy even to desperate anger of
the negro, who feel they might, at least, be the
recipient of as many favors from the women of
their own color, to say nothing of the impassible
barrier which separates him from the females of
the other race. It may well be said that the
white man is in part responsible, but true, nevertheless, and the seed of discord, dislike and hatred is taking deeper root and the races getting
further apart. This want of virtue among their
own females may be the cause of a retaliatory
sentiment in the minds of negro men, which
manifests itself in the commission of rape upon
the white women, which is sure to be followed
by a lynching, making an opportunity for the
Northern press to get in its work of exciting and
inflaming the Northern mind. We know of no
cause which tends more to increase and deepen
the hatred of this race for the whites than to
lynch one of their number for the rape of a white
woman.

Lynch one for the assassination of some victim
at the hour of midnight, for applying the torch
to the home where sleeps the mother and inno-

cent babes, or for any other capital offence of
far less magnitude, does not begin to compare in
extent of feeling aroused when one is lynched
for the rape of a white woman.   It is not infre-
quent to hear them argue thus: White men are
largely responsible for the want of virtue among
our women; a young girl of our race of comely
figure cannot escape the seductive meshes of
their passion.   If a white man rapes one of our
race it is ridiculed, but if one of us dares to
break the impassable barrier separating us, and
forces a white woman to surrender her person
to the gratification of his passion, he is sure to
die the death, and why?   Echo answers, why.
This, of course, greatly inflames the negro.

The negroes in their own midst have not the
safest advisers; while some of the things they
suffer at the hands of the whites are wrong, yet,
" It is wise to endure, what we cannot cure."
When a people are in the midst of conditions,
over which, for the present, they have no control, wisdom would teach it the best to endure,
and with patience try to correct the evil by removing the exciting cause.   Folly would endeavor to encourage the exciting cause into a
repetition of those things which so greatly offend:
the candle fly goes for the light of the candle
until he is destroyed in the flame; and we must
add, that some of the would-be wise men of their
race are guilty of grave folly, when, like Bishop

Turner, of Atlanta, Georgia, advises his people as follows:

"The fiendish lynching of John Jackson and Archibald Joiner upon mere suspicion in Louisiana, while the African Methodist-Episcopal Bishops were meeting in New Orleans, only a few miles from the scene of blood and death, was most damnable. Let every negro in this country, with a spark of manhood in him, supply his house with one, two or three guns, or with a seven or sixteen shooter, and we advise him to keep them loaded and ready for immediate use, and when his domicile is invaded by bloody lynchers, or any mob by day or night, Sabbath or week day, turn loose your missiles of death, and blow your fiendish invaders into a thousand giblets.

"We have had it in our minds to say this for seven years, but on account of our Episcopal status, we hesitated to express ourselves thus, fearing it would meet the disapproval of the House of Bishops, but their approval or disapproval has done nothing to stop the fiendish murderers who stalk abroad and are exterminating my race; so we have now said it, and hereafter we shall speak it, preach it, tell it and write it again. Again we say, get your guns negroes; get guns, and may God give you good aim when you shoot."

We say this was grave folly; not that we justify the lynchers, for we are not in the full possession of all the circumstances and facts, but grave folly for that, right or wrong, it tends to excite, inflame and madden the mind of the whites even to a degree of desperation.

We have offered in the foregoing pages of this chapter a few of the reasons, which are mutual, for the growing dislike between the two races.

We now submit a few which tend to make the white man dislike the negro.   It seems a part of his nature to make all out of his white friends his opportunities will admit, and it is frequently the case in ways which will not stand the crucial test of moral examination.

Recently we overheard a negro song, the doggerel of which runs thus:

" What's de use my workin' so hard?
  My wife works in a white man's yard :
  She cooks de chicken and saves me de wing:
  She thinks I'se workin', but I ain't doin' a thing."

It illustrates the conditions which obtain in the South better than any words of my own. We know, not only do we pay and board our cooks, but feed their families as well; this enables them to save up their earnings, buy homes and dress better than the poorer class of our white people; who, on account of the conditions obtaining in the South, which make doing this kind of work or ordinary manual labor degrading, hate the negro.   He would gladly do all work done by the negroes, the poorer class of our white women would do all the work done by the negro women, if customs would permit, but an inexorable law of society debars our poorer whites from doing certain kind of work, making it detract from their social standing and respectability. As before said, our people would gladly do all the work, our women would gladly go out to service as domestics, taking a real pleasure in a work which in turn for their reward would bring them a competent and independent living; with hands and hearts standing ready to do all work for an independent existence, they look on and see the negro race getting a monopoly of all work, making a comfortable living, supporting their families, and in many instances gathering about them little homes, while they stand helpless, ofttimes feeling the need of the subsistence they would be so willing to earn in honest toil of any kind.

As we have seen, the iron law of customs, which had its beginning with the institution of slavery, will remain with this race of people whenever and wherever they sojourn among the whites. The negro, while free, is called upon to do certain kinds of work, because the customs of slavery in a lesser degree obtains; his white employer will order him about in a manner unlike the way he would prefer to speak to a white servant; he would call upon him to do work

3

which customs forbid he should ask, or that the
white man should do.   The very custom itself is
the tap-root of a deep-seated, wide-spread and
growing hatred between the two races.   The
poor whites are wont to cry out in the agony
of their souls against a fate and custom which
gives to the interior and ex-slave race superior
advantages and opportunities of a livelihood.

As all of us know in the South, the seed of
discord is sown in the minds of the little children, and they grow up in this supreme hatred
each for the other, which increases, taken together with other reasons herein stated, widening and deepening the gulf separating the two
races.   The men of influence and wealth in the
South see these conditions; they wish it were
otherwise; and were it possible for them to bring
about a change, gladly would they do so, and·
welcome its coming.   Indeed, the negro, in a
measure, limited in extent, we trust, breaks the
harmony of concord and agreement between
these and the poorer class of whites; the latter
see these in the homes of the well-to-do, getting
work, pay and a good living, reasons himself
into a feeling of dislike for his more fortunate
white friends, in that he believes the negro is
given the preference.   But oh! how vastly mistaken they are; conditions and customs make it,
not choice.   For these, the men of influence, and
wealth would have it otherwise if it were possi-

ble; they, too, are tired of being made the common prey of this race; they are impatient with the negro's ingratitude and growing insolence; while the negroes, as their employers well know, entertain the same feeling for them they do for the poorer white brothers, and are restrained from an open exhibition of their feeling, in the fear of the loss of employment and discharge. All of us are frequently made to see evidences and unmistakable signs of the feeling this race has for the whites, in frequent occurrences, like the following: Soon after the election, when it was made certain that Major McKinley was elected President, a lady in Tarboro, N. C., went to hire a cook. She called at the home of a negro woman known to be efficient in that service, and was told, "No, indeed, madam, you cannot hire me to cook; more than that, the time is not far distant when conditions will change and we will have you for our cooks."

Sometime in the fall of 1896 a certain lady of influence and wealth was traveling in eastern North Carolina on the train, when a negro man came and demanded she give him a seat with her; he was told she would do no such thing; a negro woman just in the rear, said, "I would have that seat or die"—this, too, in violation of well-established rules of the railroad company's providing separate coaches for this race. Recently a small gathering of negroes were overheard discussing the future, in which they were heard to say, that we negroes must have a war here and clean out the white people. Ridiculous conclusion, of course, for the result of such a war would be different.

We only mention this as some evidence of feeling at present existing in the South, which will lead up in the distant future to greater evils we know not of. " Coming events cast their shadows before." We have the shadows. When we will reach the events, and how dangerous will be their proportions, none but an allwise God can tell. Of this, more will be said in another chapter.

The feeling of hatred and dislike existing in the South between the races is not confined to this generation, for the aged of our people well know and can testify that the negro has always entertained an extreme dislike, with a feeling akin to hatred, for the poorer classes of white people. This feeling is mutual. The poorer classes of whites in the days of slavery despised the negro with great bitterness of feeling, so that the soil has been in good condition from the beginning, into which the seed of discord, envy, jealousy, and even hatred has been sown and carefully cultivated by both races for bad all the while, no matter what the wishes of those who have made honest efforts to allay discord and harmonize all differences between the races. Then,

again, the Northern press has done much in sow-
ing the seed of discord, and causing this feeling of
dislike to gather volume and force in its growth
and extent; while the distinguished Wendell Phil-
lips, Bishop Gilbert Haven, and Canon George
Rawlinson have added a double measure of their
full share in widening, deepening and lengthening
the gap, even to making an abyss whose width,
depth and length cannot be measured—in advising, preaching and proclaiming that the solution
of the race problem in the South could only be
by the amalgamation of the two races. They
might as well have shaken a red flannel flag in
the face of a Spanish bull, or applied a fire brand
to a powder magazine.

How much mischief and harm such men have
done in making lines hard and difficult, not alone
for the negro, but for both races in the South,
can never be known. Near the birth of the present generation, in our State Constitutions, we
forever declared against the inter-marriage of
the races. If these celebrities could to-day pass
through our Southland, they would see our people further from their advice and preaching than
they were at the close of the war, which resulted in the negro's freedom.

We of the South believe that the amalgama-
tion of the two races is no part of God's plan.
In this we believe our Northern friends agree.
A nobler race of people, of proud inheritance,

brave men, with beautiful women, never adorned
any spot of this earth.   Possessed of virtue, intelligence, and great race pride, to say that they
would amalgamate with the negro race would
be to turn back the wheels of evolution, to stop
progress, deny all that scientists have done and
discovered in all ages, and start afresh down the
road of race degradation and ruin.   *   *   Over
the few marriages between white women and
negro men, which occasionally occur in the
North, we draw the mantle of charity, and at-
tribute such folly in white women to mental de-
rangement and temporary insanity.   No self-
respecting white woman, in the full possession
of her senses, North or South, would ever be so
lost to shame and love of race pride as to unite
herself in marriage with a negro, to become the
mother of a hybrid mulatto race.   God forbids
such a union.

While we give the negro credit for much and
believe him capable of more progressive advance-
ment, in the way of learning and civilization,
yet we know he is an inferior race, who, under
the most favorable conditions, will not and cannot ever achieve what his white friend can, because it is not the purpose of God, the great wise
Creator, that he should; then to say that the
amalgamation of the two races is the solution of
the great race problem in the South is only to
insult the virtue and intelligence of a proud peo-

ple.   Scientific investigation has shown that
amalgamation produces an inferior race.

We here call attention to and invite a careful
perusal of that able work, by Prof. Alexander
Winchell, LL. D., " The Preadamites." If any
such there be in this country, or in any land now,
who fear that the white people of the South will
amalgamate with the negro, let him put fears
forever to sleep, never again to awake. Our children and children's children are being taught
the dangerous consequences of such a course to
posterity. Let it be here said to the credit of the
negroes that they are as jealous of the pure blood
of their race, and as a people guard the teachings
of the rising generation against such practices.

We have seen some of the reasons in the foregoing pages, which was the beginning, growth
and extension of the great and impassible sea
which divides these two people.   In presenting
these, a careful effort has been made to be just
and truthful. In the succeeding chapters of this
work we will endeavor to point out what must
appear to advanced thinkers as the only true solution of the race problem in the South.

CHAPTER III.

" CAN WE COLONIZE THE NEGRO ? "

The answer to this query depends largely upon three important questions:

First, and most important of these, is the amount of interest the white race of the United States will take in the work of colonization.

Second. The plan of colonization and the means used in effecting it.

Third. The place or territory wherein it is proposed to colonize them.

The consideration of the first and third will be found in other chapters of this work.

We have seen in the previous chapter some evidence of a disposition in the negro to congregate and live in exclusion of other races. This, we think, is obedient to natural laws and instincts. A saying that " birds of a feather will flock together " is appropos here. The author of these words certainly understood the natural tendencies of all known living creatures. His poetry had certainly as much, if not more, of common sense, observation and experience as it has of rhyme. Every species of animal creation observe strictly this law of nature, and in this we mean not only animals, but the fowl of the air and the fishes of the sea as well. Take, for instance, animals of the same genus but differing in species, left undisturbed they would never interbreed; nor would they ever associate and mingle in companionship, each with the other. The same is true of the human family; if observent of nature's instincts and tendencies, they would never hybridize. We feel sure that the negro, obedient to natural instincts, would like to assemble together in exclusion of all others, in some place wherein they could live solely, separately and alone. In this does he differ from our observation of the experience of other members of the human family? Do we not see the Israelites, while scattered over the face of the earth, gathering themselves together in little colonies, in those towns where they happen to be, living to themselves socially, inter-marrying with none but their own race? This people, throughout the world, are to-day forming themselves into societies and planning their return to Palestine. The Jews are with us, but not of us. Their desire to return to their native land is in conformity to natural laws, which are Divine, and therefore obedient to the will of God. Go to the city of New York and other large cities, and we find the German settlements, Chinatown, Italian quarters, and on to the end of the catalogue. Like the Gulf stream in the sea of waters, still maintaining their separate and distinct identity.

We have given in the foregoing some reasons showing the tendencies of this race, like all others, to congregate and live together in exclusion of other people. There is little reason to doubt the willingness of this people to embrace any favorable opportunity to colonize, under the auspices of this government. No well developed plan, of which the author has any knowledge, extensive in detail, has been given to the public, looking to the separation of the two races and the colonization of the negro. It is true, we believe, some have hinted or suggested colonization in some of the South American States, also in Arizona and in New Mexico of the United States. We do not think that any proposed plan of colonization of this race in any unfavored section should be entertained, however, the place suited and the reasons for its selection will be found in another chapter. In this chapter the plan and possibility of colonization are discussed.

Let the general Government purchase some favored section of the country, open up the land for entry in small homesteads to each settler, and make appropriations, small of course, to each family with which to aid in getting about them the necessaries of life, with which to start. It would probably be well to charge a small sum, according to value, for the land entered, to be paid for at some time in the future, making the time long and the payments small; then have

the residents of other States to make no sale of
land to this race, but, by moral suasion and all
other fair and legitimate means, endeavor to get
them to migrate to the section of country set
apart for their special benefit. Let it be a part
of the work of the whites to point out to this
race the good results which must flow to them
from permanent colonization.

At the same time, present to their minds in a
forceful way the great and disastrous consequences which must come at some time in the
future, from continued existence together of the
two races within the same boundary, contributing much to the great work by withholding employment. We believe that the negro would
gladly embrace the opportunity and begin at
once to move out from among his white friends,
on account of the appreciable reasons already
given, and which will more elaborately be discussed in other chapters of this work.

Among other causes, which would induce the
negro to settle by themselves are his great love
of power, his desire and ambition to rule, which
he well knows he can never do among the whites;
his love for the unity of his people, their natural
disposition, which we have already seen, is to
live together in exclusion of other races.

Their evident dislike of the white people, with
whom they have already lived a generation, on
account of the mutual hatred existing between

this race and the poorer classes of whites, who
are in the majority. The thoughtful of his race
are as much perplexed over the race problem in
the South as are the whites. While much regretted by the better class of negroes, they know
that it is only necessary for time to culminate
this great problem, greater than all issues con-
cerning our welfare, into a solution, freighted
with awful consequences to both people. We
wish to emphasize the fact that it is regretted,
deeply so, by the thoughtful of both races, but,
notwithstanding these regrets, the handwriting
is seen upon the wall. This true, the leaders of
this race would, we think, act in concert with
the people of this country, having their well-
being at heart, induce the negroes to migrate to
the section bought and set apart by the general
government for them, with appropriate assistance to start them in their new home; especially
so, if the general government would have a su-
perintending, paternal care over them, in the formation of that government best suited to their
new conditions. Surely this assistance, advisory
and helpful in the formation of their government,
substantial and material, in getting about them
the means and ways of an existence, would be
freely given by all good people of this country,
of which class it is hoped our legislators and
statesmen are made.

The good will of the people of the United

States, and certainly, too, of the South, which would be measured not only in wishes but in deeds and substance, the negro would take with him in his new home.

The race feeling, we have seen in the preceding chapter, existing in the South, the natural tendencies of all races to live in exclusion of others, the proposed plan of the government to help him in securing homes and paternally advising and assisting in the formation of his plan of government, the dangers which they must see through the mist of years towards humanity of both races in the South, the results of such a conflict in the survival of the fittest and strongest, and conversely the destruction of the weaker, can have, we think, but one effect, the hearty approval of the opportunities of gathering together this people in some favored clime, separate and apart from all others, where alone and undisturbed, they may serenely enjoy the glory of that power, peace and prosperity which the friends of this race hope for them in the years to come, when a full opportunity, if ever is given, to exemplify to the world their ability.

CHAPTER IV.

THE NEGRO'S CAPACITY FOR SELF-GOVERNMENT AND SEPARATE EXISTENCE.

We have no sufficient data, drawn from actual experience of any civilized and intelligent race of negroes, in modern times—there are no such. · We are driven, then, to speak from observation and experience of those we know something of.

Our knowledge of the habits, customs and ways of the Southern negro is such as to teach us to expect a favorable answer to the query. In those sections of the Southern States wherein this race are largely in the majority—for instance, in Mississippi, Louisiana and Alabama, the negro becomes large land-owners, good farmers, prosperous and successful.

Taking a comparison made between contiguous counties wherein the blacks are largely in the majority in the one, the whites in the other, we find the taxable value of the property largely favorable to the negro.   Again, considering the whole State, in any one wherein this race outnumbers all others and comparison made, at least, shows that the black States hold their own in point of prosperity, the condition of the people at least as good as are found in those States wherein the whites are largely in the majority.

They maintain in these negro settled States, schools of a high order, successfully managed by their own race. The reader's attention is invited to an examination of the work done at Shaw University and St. Augustine College, North Carolina; Claflin University, South Carolina; Alcorn and other colleges in Mississippi, and other higher institutions of learning in Alabama, Georgia and other Southern States.

Human nature is such that all of us will make more desperate efforts in our own service than we will in the service of others.

Colonized alone, with their own little farms to cultivate, homes to improve, we would find this people, not unlike others, but desirous of succeeding in the race of life, changing from an idle laborer, if such a contradictory term may ever be used, into a selfish property gatherer. They would be possessed by a spirit of emulation and rivalry, which at all times is a great incentive, to say nothing of the selfish desire of the power which money and property brings, common to not a few of all mankind. Colonized they see the possibilities of greater success of becoming the owner of large fields, of broad acres, that which they cannot easily have among their white friends. It is true, however, as we have seen, he can more surely and certainly, on account of conditions in the South, about which we have heretofore spoken, more easily buy and pay for

little homes and dress better than the poorer
classes of whites in the towns. Yet the opportunities of getting farms, certainly of any size
among the whites, is out of the question, for the
reason that such places are not for sale to him,
besides he has but little ambition to accumulate
more than his home, for that money and property, under present conditions, cannot buy for
him power and influence.

Another thing which would greatly aid the
colonized negroes would be the genuine and sincere assistance which all Christian and good people in this country will render them. The children and grandchildren of slave owners still
have traditionary notions of fondness for this
race, and in their new home they would be the
recipients of the kindness and good will which
they now have, and we insist, in a larger degree,
for that the exciting tendencies of race feeling,
to abate his willing action, will be removed with
them in the distance. More than that, the plain
people, or, perhaps, more expressive, the poorer
classes of white people, would so welcome the
coming of the plan of separation by colonization,
that, notwithstanding their great bitterness of
feeling, about which we have heretofore spoken
in other chapters, they would gladly and willingly pay the taxes now so grudgingly given
for the education of this race, to aid and assist
them in their new homes, removed from conflict

with them in the industrial race, constituting no longer a barrier to their success. Then the Northern friends of this race, always disposed to aid them, could, with less restraint, carry on their work of assistance. All of this we are fully persuaded would stimulate the negro to greater deeds and efforts to succeed and be like his white neighbors, especially when his missionary white friends, from all parts, interested in his success and well-being, would come among them, teach, and show them the ways of life. Race pride would play no inconspicuous part in urging them onward to success; aware that the eye of the world would center its gaze, critically too, upon them, would be an incentive which would stir them both in mental and physical activity; knowing well that thousands of expectant friends anxiously, but hopefully awaited the results of their own experience, would inspire them under their new condition to great efforts.

We now come to consider the negroes' capacity for self-government. This, too, will be experimental; we are aware that many there are, who will insist that this race is incapable of making or creating any government founded upon Christian example and moral precept, managed in an enlightened and civilized manner, for the greatest good of their people. We are aware that there are those who insist that this people, left by themselves, would relapse into barbarism and the benighted practices of their Afric ancestors. We are aware that many insist that this people would not exist save and except in a state of barbaric life, as did his ancestors in his native land, if he had not the plenteous barn and smokehouse of his white friend to go to.

The valuable lessons of their slave ancestors. learned while in touch with their white masters, and in turn handed down to their posterity, that thirty-two years of education of the present generation. learned in the presence of the white man, with the benefits of the directing influence of their salutary example. would serve them no good purpose, if colonized. and left alone to work out the problem of their own race existence. We admit that what the Southern negroes are the white race of the South have made them; it is true that if they are anything. it is the result of the training and education by example and precept of their white friends as well as the learning had in the school-room.

We know that the negro is an imitative creature, for that matter. who is not? and living with the white people he is constantly doing whatever he sees his white friends do. We are not forgetful that the best way of teaching is by example. We are not forgetful that to remove him would deprive this people of much in this way; then he would be driven to the necessity of independent action and thought; and our enquiry in the remaining pages of this chapter, is the ability and capacity of this race for independent action. We differ with those who are of this mind. We believe the negro, colonized in some favorable section in the Southern part of the United States, in touch with the Christian civilization, and where the government can have over him a parental, supervising care, would give to the world a surprising demonstration of his capacity to manage his own affairs.

Certainly we do not mean to convey the idea that he would offer to the world any conspicuous example of government worthy of emulation in the beginning during the first years of their new history, for who would expect that of this race? This we mean, that left alone, taking with him the education and training of a generation, and in easy reach of the white man's government, whom he has shown a disposition in other matters to imitate; this people would satisfy the world of their ability, not only to prosper and get ahead in the management of living and property getting, but like ability to govern themselves. Were they not in the remote ages of antiquity in civilization and enlightenment, in advance of all people? Does not ancient history prove that, "when Asia was a land of tents and shepherds, Greece a waste, Rome a desert, and the western continent unknown in song and story, Africa rose the proud mother of nations and the

central source of civilization and social refine-
ment ? "

We know, those of us who have given the matter any thought, that the negroes' environments
check and curb their ambition; they know that
education to them is only useful to the extent of
learning to read and write and make figures;
beyond this they have no incentive; for that
the 'best they can hope to do, and the limit of
their ambition, is to teach in the common schools,
with an occasional chance of becoming a little
prominent, with his own people, as a minister
of the Gospel. They know that in the field of
possibilities open to white men, they have not
and will not be permitted to enter. Colonized,
with the rights of self-government, at once you
open up a new world to them, they see the possibilities of greatness, in the realms of science and
higher education; open to them the way to a seat
in the United States Senate and in the halls of
Congress, chances of Governorship, Judgeship,
and all the offices innumerable in the system of
State government; at once you inspire them to
greater deeds; they would call upon the latent
energies of their being to gratify their ambition;
they would put into the work the utmost and
best strength of their nature; emulation and
rivalry would play their best role, in a word,
with them colonized in States, with a right of
self-government, they would find all the ave-

nues of greatness in the professions and all things
open to him that are open to the whites in other
sections. The love of power and influence, which
comes with the position, the influence which
money and property brings would have full play
upon their inspiration for nobler and greater
efforts to acquire them.

We have some evidence of the negroes' capacity to govern and organize among us; we know
that their church organizations are superb. We
will pause here to say that this race love their
church. They are religious, and wait upon the
ordinances of their church with almost idolatrous
pleasure. The will of the pastor is supreme, if
worthy, and they have confidence in him. No
emperor ever had greater influence over his people than they have over their flocks. All of us
know the power of their political organizations;
no people or party have given a greater examples of perfect political organizations than we
have, in this race of people in the South, except
in those sections of the South where State Constitutions impose qualification to suffrage, or the
right of ballot.

Their Burial Societies are managed with con-
summate success. In this they set an example
which the whites, and especially the poorer
whites, might well follow. Their lodges, in so
far as the public have any knowledge, are as
well managed as the lodges and secret orders of

the whites. We know that in those sections wherein he is thickly settled, and especially in those sections where they live in entire exclusion of almost all others, those who own their homes are the best citizens. and wield a powerful influence for good. From this is adduced the argument. that those who get property, either among us or when colonized, would make an effort for the protection of themselves and their possessions, as well as for others who own property, to have good government.

We have seen in another chapter the plan of colonization would be to interest all in good government by making them property owners, opening up entries of homestead to them at little or no cost, becoming owners of their homes would at once beget in them the desire of good government for the protection of home and family.

Those of us who think it well for the good of posterity and the future of our Southern country, forming no inconsiderable part of this Union, in which every citizen of this nation should feel a great interest without regard to section, that the negro should be colonized, have never at any time entertained the thought of sending them into a State of separate existence, without sending with him, not only the good will and best wishes for their success. of our people, but those capable of teaching and willing to instruct him in the art of self-government. The friends of the negro would desire that the general Government shall take a part in the formation of their State government, at least until he has become accustomed to and practiced in the ways of governing and directing the affairs of State. The friends of this race, both North and South, would wish the general Government to furnish him substantial aid. not only in the art of governing. but in the more practical and needful lessons of living and earning a separate and independent existence.

There are good people in all sections of this country, patriotic men and women inspired by love of humanity, as well as their love of country, who would be willing to give of their means and time in helping and teaching this race of people in their new homes the ways of good government and moral life. The world never has seen a more marked example of encouragement, sincere and well meant, even to the point of rendering material aid and substantial assistance by neighboring people of another race, than the negro would have. as a people, in their new and colonized home. The nation would wish their success because they would form a part of this nation of people. This nation would do all possible to aid and encourage them in the field of industrial development, in making them useful and good citizens; in short. it would be to the interest of the United States to have them succeed, for our nation would be strong or weak just in the proportion to the prosperity, happiness and success of its whole people.

Under these conditions we believe verily that the negro is capable and would manage his own affairs if put alone in some favored section, with the kindly assistance of their white friends.

Another sign of encouragement is that the more intelligent and advanced thinkers of his people are beginning to have a race pride, and are looking towards the elvation of their people.

The love of power and influence which follows the possessions of wealth and intelligence, the encouragement they would receive from their white friends, the aid and assistance which this nation would give them, would be an incentive to great efforts, and greater than all this, that which would more influence the intelligent and thoughtful of this race would be the knowledge, that not only the nation but the eyes of the world would with interest watch their success or failure; this more than all else would bring into play the latent energies and capabilities of this once great race. The satisfaction and pleasure of disappointing and surprising those who see for this people only failure, and the satisfaction their success would afford their friends, and those who believe them capable would be a powerful, inciting cause of action, sufficient to bring into use all the ability this people possess.

We cannot conclude this chapter without an appeal to critics to forbear. We do not know the possibilities of this race, and therefore ask for them a stay of the tongue, which will utter any sentiment tending to discourage them, when the idea of colonization has, as it certainly will, take possession of this people, when the matter is agitated.

Not alone will it take possession of this race, but we are confident when we come to think seriously upon the matter, that we, too, will be possessed with the idea of a separation as the best thing for the good of both races in the South.

CHAPTER V.

THE NEGRO A BARRIER TO INDUSTRIAL PROGRESS.

It has long been evident to the enquiring that the presence of the negro in the South is a real mountain in the way of Southern prosperity, enterprise and progress.

With fertile lands, broad rivers, magnificent forests, rich in mineral resources, salubrious climate, the South is not making the strides along the roadway of prosperity and progress which might be expected of her. We have said the negro is a barrier, an obstacle of mountainous proportion in the road of Southern progress. It is with no intention on their part that this is true, but it is true, nevertheless. Experience and observation teaches, that not many more than one-half of the people of the South are actually employed in any profitable work. Of this idle class there are as many of one race as there are of the other, though not in proportion to the numerical strength of each people. There are as many idle white people as there are negroes, not more. While the white population of the ten Southern States (Virginia, North Carolina, South Carolina, Georgia, Florida, Alabama, Mississippi, Louisiana, Texas and Arkansas), was, in 1890, eight million three hundred thousand. The ne-

gro population of the same States at the same
time was five million eight hundred thousand,
about fifty per cent of both sex of the negro
race are idlers. There are as many idle whites,
but not fifty per cent of the population. This
candid statement will greatly astonish, no doubt,
our Northern friends, who are trained to industrious habits of useful employment from their
childhood. What is the reason for this? There
is a cause for every effect; we have the effect,
and see indolent, idle men and women (both races) throughout the South. Where and what is
the cause? Are the white people of the South
by nature indolent and lazy? The author will
never make that admission. He would not so
slander the brave sons and beautiful daughters
of the people from whom he descended, and with
whom he first saw the light of day, and among
whom he has spent all the days of his life.

Well, what is the cause? First, let's speak
of the idle negro and the cause of his indolence.
The negro, by reasons of certain conditions and
environments is not over anxious to work. His
efficiency as a laborer we will speak of in another
part of this chapter. They know, through the
kind indulgence and lax ways of their more fortunate white friends, whether they work or
play, they will obtain a subsistence. Dealing
with facts and truths, we are constrained to say
that a part of their creed and training even from

childhood is to learn ways and means to get all from the white man they possibly can, and give in return for the same just as little as they can. This feeling generates idleness among them, in many ways, particularly this: The few employed, religiously practicing the lessons of faith and childhood training, get all for their labor possible from the white man, and then add to this store all else in their way, he is able to support a half-score in idleness, which they seem to take a great pleasure in doing. They can, when willing, live on as little as any other people, and by grouping make the expense of house rent almost nothing. This condition is not true in as large a degree in the rural districts as in the cities and towns.

We will pause here to say this habit of idleness with the negro race would be cured, if removed from his white friends and thrown on his own personal resouces, it would then be root pig or die poor, the pig would root. All the world knows that the natural inclinations of all living creatures is to live in ease and idleness, and the proportion of idle time, is just in proportion to the providence of other means for an existence and support. Man is no exception to this rule, and it is certain the negro is not. Just as long as the few employed, being mainly parents and older ones, can care for and support this hord of unemployed in their idleness, then the conditions above spoken of will continue to exist. When

this people come to know that, from their own
corn-crib and smoke-house they must live, a great
change will come over the spirit of their dreams;
in good weather they will be seen preparing for
the storm that is to come, the fifty per cent of
the unemployed will be seen with the plow,
shovel and hoe, axe and saw, using their brawn
and muscle in honest effort to provide support
for themselves and their dependents. It is true
in a large degree the white people are responsible
for these conditions.

In the days of slavery, slave owners were in
the habit of trusting much of their business, and
especially the farm and labor, to the management of their slaves, who, in many instances,
were faithful and good managers; their owners
became careless and enjoyed their leisure, letting
affairs take care of themselves, in a sort of hap-
py-go-lucky style.

The examples of parents leave its impress upon
the children, generation after generation, even
to the present, have imbibed and practiced these
careless habits of business; the results are as is
always the case. We have an inefficient system
of labor and laborers, in no way comparing with
the labor of our Northern and Western friends.

The experience of all people teach that labor
left to look after itself is poor labor; moreover,
having the full opportunities, entrusted with the
management of affairs, he makes the best of it,

not always particular and scrupulously exact in
the returns he makes to his employer. From
this we see that conditions in the South, tending
to demoralize labor and at the same time giving
opportunity to the few employed, whose moral
education, for want of time, is not up to the
standard, to add largely to the supplies which
his wages would buy, enabling him to keep in
idleness a horde of unemployed about him. Then,
is it surprising that our people of the South are
slow in the way of progress and enterprise.

For a while now we will see the other side of
the picture. We have said, that there are as
many idle whites in the Southern States as tnere
are idle negroes, and in a large majority of instances, the idle of the whites are poorly off in
this world's goods, and could not afford to live a
life of idleness. We have said, also, that these
are not idle through choice, but so from conditions surrounding them. In all sections where
slavery obtains menial work is considered degrading, and none but slaves are called upon
or expected to do the baser sort of labor. These
conditions sprung up in the South with the beginning of slavery; the white man or woman
who went out to service in the capacity of a
common laborer, were esteemed no better than
the slavish negro. However foolish it may seem,
it is nevertheless verily true, as any can prove
who care to put themselves to the trouble. The

result was and now is that the poorer classes of
white people will eke out a miserable existence
at home, if they are fortunate enough to have
such, rather than go into service as cooks, house-
maids and the like; or men as laborers, because
the work is considered degrading—it is the func-
tion of the negro. In order to be respected, I
cannot and must not do a negroes' work. Gold,
even at high prices, will not hire our white girls
for cooks and house-maids, although at home
they have a scant existence, with clothes not the
best. Oh, no, that is the negroes work, and I am
better than a negro; and while in need of better
dresses and a better filled larder, still I cannot
afford to put myself upon a common level with
the negro; foolish condition it is true, but it is
true notwithstanding. All of us here in the South
know they are not so much to blame, for work
does degrade and detract from one's social standing. The class of the South who suffer most,
perhaps, because of this inexorable law of society, is largely the aristocracy of the land. For
generation after generation, their ancestry were
wealthy and large slave owners; children born,
raised in the belief that work formed no part of
the plan of their existence. All of this swept
away by the war, finding themselves poor indeed,
they have continued in the same state, not rally-
ing, not recuperating their fortunes for the one
and only reason; the little mite left, and all

they have earned, is paid out to negro servants, in order that the daughters and young men may keep their hands from the degrading employment of work. Now will any one be unkind enough to say, these are not willing to work; not so, gladly would they better their condition by honest toil, but for that inexorable and ironclad law of our social fabric, which makes work disreputable. For shame! for shame! that thirty-two years of struggle and hardship since the smoke of battle cleared away, since the boys who wore the blue and grey laid down their arms and became friends, and yet our poverty-stricken people have not lived down these foolish conditions and adjusted themselves to the wants and needs of a people struggling to rebuild their fortunes. The belief that labor degrades, added to this, the indisposition of the more fortunate whites, to see white servants put in the same position and ordered around as negroes, is the cause and means which make in the South as many idle white people as there are idle negroes, not idle from choice, but for reasons which they cannot control. No people on earth can prosper and do well, nor accumulate wealth among whom such things exist, with no well directed efforts, we are sorry to say, to prevent it.

Another barrier to Southern development, growing out of the presence of the negro, is, as we have seen in another chapter, the results of

intense feeling existing between the two races,
tending to keep and actually keeping emigrants
and capital away from us. We have seen that
the Northern press, using as the means the occasional lawless outbreaks in the South which
sometimes result in lynching, to inflame the
Northern mind, the effect of which is to frighten
persons of small means from coming among us
and investing their small fortunes, in the belief
that they are resting upon a slumbering volcano,
which at some unexpected moment may explode
in an outbreak between the two races, sweeping
away their little all and possibly endangering
life itself. A separation of the two races will remove the exciting cause, lynching would stop,
the press could no longer flaunt the signal of danger in the face of would-be settlers and investors,
and a land so blessed by nature's bounteous gifts,
would become the home wherein the fortunes of
so many would be made.

Separation of the two races would cause the
countless thousands of unemployed whites, gladly to engage in the very work done by this people.
While they in their new homes would engage in
useful employment as a necessity to existence,
being removed from the storehouse and assistance of their indulgent white friends.

It is therefore not difficult to see the results
which follow. Labor always finds its reward;
the employment of the whites would result in

5

bettering their condition in every way, giving them homes, farms, honest employment, and in the orderly course of things, fortunes. With happy homes and plenty, the result and reward of industry, comes power, wealth and greatness to the State.

Contrast this with the other view, an idle people, with young men and young women without honest employment, with but poor if any home, less comforts, presenting the appearance of shabby genteel, not enough of cash to indulge them in the simplest necessities of life, makes a weak people, makes a people without power and influence, the ambition and spirit of success goes out. Fortunes are seldom if ever made, a competency for their offspring only to a few; and this view is what is seen all through the South, especially in those parts where the negro forms a conspicuous part of the population.

We have heard some insist that the South cannot get on without them, being the only labor. What a mistake:

First. Not more than fifty per cent of this race are employed.

Second. For every idle negro man and woman in the South there is an idle white man and woman; not idle from choice, who would be willing and glad to take the place and do the work done, if this race could be sent into colonization, thus removing the degrading notions, that white peo-

ple must not do the negroes' kind or sort of work.
So that, if it were possible to remove him bodily
and at once, we have those holding their hands
in discontented idleness, and enough ready and
willing to fill his place without feeling the loss
at all.

We have already said that he is not a good laborer. Of course this statement must be quali-
fied, for that it does not apply to all; there are
exceptions; some of them are very good workers,
with commendable fidelity try to earn their employers money in doing good service; the majority are not good laborers; they are careless
and indifferent, oftimes doing the work in hand
more harm than service, always needing some
one to urge them onward and see to it that their
work is properly done.

We have already discussed the reasons for this,
and see that for much of his inefficiency, as a
laborer, the white man is responsible. Send them
into colonization, and we believe the whole
South, including their colonized territory, will
start upon a new era of prosperity. They in their
new home will work to make comfortable and
happy their own possessions. What a volume of
meaning this sentence takes with it, to improve
one's possessions. They would be made self-reliant, and we verily believe, and hope will become
better and more useful citizens. Certainly we
think their morals would improve, for then the

great temptation to relieve their white friends of
a part of their belongings, excusing their con-
science in that they helped at least to make it,
would be removed. We think, also, the virtue
of the young women would be better guarded.
It would be the pride of the better class of this
race to use all possible means for the betterment
of their moral condition. The knowledge of the
fact that the eyes of all mankind are upon them,
is the most powerful incentive to greater action,
in the hope of winning applause, that is known.

We will conclude this chapter by contrasting
the condition of the farmers and people, in the
western and mountainous sections of the Southern States, where they are to be found only few
in number, with the eastern and cotton sections,
and in and near the cities and towns, where he
forms a conspicuous part of the population,
oftimes largely in the majority. In the former
we find the farming people out of debt, most of
them with some money, sometimes money lend-
ers; whereas , in the negro sections, we find the
farmers in debt, heavily mortgaged, and increasing their mortgages each year. What is the
cause of this ? There are two reasons. In the
former, the hand that grasps the dollar is the
hand that made it, by working for it; whereas,
in the latter, farms are too large, but chiefly,
one white man will wear the seat of his pants
threadbare in the shade of a tree watching two

negroes, not specially interested in his success, doing what he might, with applied energy and muscle, himself do.   The former works hard upon his own lands, and settles with himself for the labor done.   The latter does not work at all, while the negro laborers, accustomed to the careless and not over-exacting ways of his white friends, work poorly.   Suppose you take from him his two negro laborers, send them upon lands of their own, and he takes hold with brawn and muscle and does the work himself, that which he has been in the habit of hiring done.   What would be the result?   Each of the negroes on his own land would do good work, putting forth their best efforts to improve their homes and earn a support for those dependent upon them, while the family of the man with threadbare pants would witness an era of prosperity, enjoying comforts and luxuries to them before unknown; instead of paying double wages for not the best of labor, with improved farming implements, brain and muscle, he would do the work and settle with himself for the labor.

CHAPTER VI.

THE BURDEN OF EDUCATING THE NEGRO RACE TOO GREAT FOR THE SOUTH ALONE.

Another strong argument favoring the separation of the two races in the South and the colonization of the negro, is, we think, the matter of education.

Our Southern folk have acted a noble part in this work. With fortunes swept away by the ravages of war, with millions of slaves made free, clad with all the habiliment of citizenship, densely ignorant of their rights as such, unfitted for the new conditions, our people set themselves to work to remove the pall of ignorance overhanging this race, and prepare them by education to properly appreciate and use all rights and privileges given them by President Lincoln's Proclamation. We have spoken of this in another chapter of this work. It is, however, our purpose here to enlarge upon what has already been said.

No people on earth ever acted more nobly than did our people of the Southern States with regard to negro education. By Mr. Lincoln's proclamation this race of people, who for generations had been their slaves and their property, were made citizens with equal rights before the law. All

history does not give a more conspicuous example of forbearance without murmur, of a more
willing and ready adjustment to new conditions.
The people of the South set themselves to work
to repair their broken fortunes, to educate their
own children and the children of their old slaves.
Our State Constitutions were remodeled to suit
the new conditions.   What a monument of glory
to the generosity of the hearts of our Southern
folk, to bind ourselves and our posterity to educate the children of a slave race.   The yoke of
this burden was self-placed upon our neck.   Our
people felt kindly to the old slave. He had stood
a faithful sentinel, guarding the homes of our
mothers, wives and daughters while the boys in
grey were upon the battle field of Virginia fighting to perpetuate his slavery. Then, too, he had
an affectionate regard for his master, his wife,
and their children.   The old nurses had been as
faithful in raising the children of their mistress,
as they had been raising their own and loved
them as well. We assumed the burden willingly,
imposed the tax which the whites then and now
almost exclusively pay, for the education of his
child as well as our own.   The burden was a
great one, but like true men we carried it and
paid the tax, not grudgingly, but with a willing
and open hand.   Then there was another reason
which prompted the people of the South; we felt
that the best results flow from a trained and ed-

ucated citizenship. The fabric of the criminal law excused no one of crime on the score of ignorance. Justice demanded that the citizen made amenable to the law for crime, should be educated in the knowledge of the law, which punished for crime, that he might know the thing is forbidden and learn obedience to the law.

Responsive to the demands of justice, to enlighten an ignorant people, to fit them for citizenship, to give them an understanding of our institutions, to acquaint them with the law and the ways to observe it; as Christians, to prepare them for religious truths, and to teach them that good citizenship consisted in obedience to official requirements; to love the form of government under which they lived, was the task our people willingly took upon themselves, and have faithfully discharged the responsibilities thereof.

We do not mean to be forgetful of the assistance rendered in negro education in the South by our Northern friends, both in furnishing teachers and means to build school houses, and establishing larger institutions of learning, which is a monument to their generosity and Christian purpose.

In speaking of the disposition of the Southern people to negro education, W. J. Harris, Commissioner of Education, in his able report for 1894—1895, on page 1332, says: " It is a fact well known, that almost the entire burden of

negro education in the South falls upon the white
property owners of the former slave States.   Of
the more than seventy-five million dollars expended in the past twenty years for the instruc-
tion of the colored children in the Southern public schools, but a small per cent was contributed
by the negroes themselves, in the way of taxes.
This vast sum has not been given grudgingly.
The white people of the South believe that the
State should place a common school education
within the reach of every child; and they have
done this much, to give all citizens, white and
black, an even start in life."

These are just words of praise, and the people
of the South thank you, Mr. Commissioner Harris, for them.

It is estimated that of the former sixteen slave
States. composed of Delaware, Maryland, Virginia, West Virginia, Kentucky, Tennessee,
North Carolina, South Carolina, Georgia, Florida. Alabama, Mississippi. west of the Mississippi,
Missouri, Arkansas, Lousiana and Texas, twenty-
seven per cent of all school revenues are expended in the education of the negro children.   It
will be remembered, however, that the negro
race forms only a small part of the population
of many of these States. That when we consider
those States wherein the population is nearly
evenly divided between the two races, then we
find the public school revenues, instead of being

twenty seven per cent for this race, is fifty per cent, and in some instances more. In short, always divided, with, we believe, only one exception. pro rata, according to the respective number of children of each race. Take, for instance, the State of Mississippi. White children of school age. 212,700; colored, 309,800; Louisiana—white, 203,400; colored, 216,700; South Carolina—white, 171,600; colored, 288,100 (here we find much over fifty per cent of the public school revenue goes to the education of the negro children, while in Alabama and Georgia nearly fifty per cent; in North Carolina and Florida, forty per cent; Virginia, forty and a third per cent; in Texas and Arkansas, thirty-three and a third per cent. These statistics are given that it may be seen in those sections of the South wherein the negro is most populous, is imposed upon the whites the almost incalculable burden of educating the children of a propertyless race of people who pay no taxes.

Commissioner Harris shows that in these States seventy-five to eighty million dollars have been expended in the education of the colored children since 1876 to the school year of 1893-1894. It is estimated upon the same basis for the years of 1894-1895, 1895-1896, 1896-1897 twenty millions more will be added since 1876, making one hundred million dollars that has been spent in negro education. Taking the census reports of

school age in 1894 as a basis of the 2,723,720 negro children of school age in the sixteen Southern States, 1,965,600 live in the States of Virginia, North Carolina, South Carolina, Georgia,
Alabama, Mississippi and Louisiana, about three-
fourths of the total, making these eight States,
of the one hundred million dollars pay seventy-
five million dollars. Texas and Arkansas have
done their part too. In these States there are,
in Texas, 212,500 negro children of school age—
Arkansas, 124,500, at the same ratio. Texas has
paid about eight millions, Arkansas about four
millions in the work of educating this race,
while the six other former slave States (Missouri,
Delaware, Maryland, Kentucky, Tennessee and
West Virginia) have paid only thirteen million
dollars. These figures are not accurate, but are
approximately correct. Who, then, will say that
the matter of educating this race should be left
alone to the Southern people.

The proclamation of President Lincoln, speaking for the people of this Union, made the slaves
free. By amendment to our Constitution he was
made a citizen of the United States and the State
wherein he resides, with all the rights, privileges
and protection under the law enjoyed by other
citizens—indeed, made equal before the law with
all men. We insist that in the beginning the
public burden of educating this race should have
been shared among the whole people of this

Union. Certainly, since we have, unaided, for a whole generation sustained the burden of educating this race. We of the South believe we have discharged our duty, and that now and from this time onward the whole people of the United States should be taxed for the education of the negro children. The people of the South never for one moment would ask to be relieved and discharged from their proportionate share of this burden, but do ask in equity and justice that the people of other sections contribute by taxation their share of this obligation. We believe that when the well-meaning and thoughtful make an equitable and just examination of the situation, they can reach but one conclusion, and that is, that this race made free by the people of the United States, should be the wards of this nation. That the South, having for a generation faithfully furnished the revenues for the education of this propertyless race, the time has now come when the task of lifting from them the pall of ignorance should be the work and care of the whole nation; that every citizen of the United States, every foot of soil and every dollar should bear its just proportion of this burden.

No one would think for a moment that the plan would work well for the general Government to make an appropriation of the money to be expended in negro education living among the whites, there would be jarring friction and

troubles innumerable, bad enough soon to destroy
any movement like this made for the sole benefit
of a race living at the same time upon the same
soil with another race of people. Then how
should it be done, and what is the plan? Colonize the negro; place these people to themselves,
and then you have at once solved the difficulty.
The general Government then could make an appropriation of money to be used in the education
of this race of people, limited only to the States
and territory wherein they are colonized; then
have the State wherein they are now thickly settled, so amend their Constitution as to give to
the children of the negro race only the school
fund gathered from the taxes levied upon the
property owned by this race, the effect would at
once be felt. From such States, after the Constitutions have been amended as suggested, for
want of means to educate their children, for let
it be said the negro likes to go to school. The emigration movement would at once take possession
of them, and ere long the purpose intended would
be accomplished, this people would gather themselves together in their own dominion, where
they could receive the benefit of the appropriation for the education of their children, and other
purposes which the people of the United States,
through their Congress, would, we believe, most
generously and liberally give. The sum of this
appropriation cannot be accurately given, by es-

timation we believe between six and eight million dollars are expended annually in the former slave States in educating the children of this race. What part of this sum added to the sum of the taxes gathered from these negro colonized States cannot be fairly estimated. The author is not wedded to any plan of his own for obtaining the money necessary to aid these people colonized, in their education; if by direct tax the result would be better, then let us have that which is best. We believe, however, aid through Congress would be by far the better plan. The main object aimed at, is the equalization of this burden among all the people of the Union. We believe that all people will admit the justice of the claim of the South, that the expense of educating this race should be borne by all the people of the United States alike. It was the act of the Union, the work of the nation in liberating the slave; the South was not only deprived of his property value, but for a generation have alone borne the burden of his public education. We insist, in the beginning, that the education of this race should have been the work of the nation. If it be true that this claim was then just, how much more must it be now.

There are many good people throughout the North who thought this demand a reasonable one, and proved their faith in the large and generous donations given in many sections for the establishment of many institutions for their education.

Inspired by the generous action of the South, aforementioned in this chapter, the splendid efforts made in the face of grave difficulties, the self-imposed burden in the midst of their great poverty, incident to the war resulting in the liberation of the slaves, we believe that the well-meaning men of the Northeast and West would respond in their hearts and minds, "Yes, that it is only just, fair and equitable that this property-less class of people who, as slaves, were liberated by this nation without compensation to his owner, the burden of whose education, for a generation has been borne by the Southern people alone, should now become the task and burden of the whole people of this Union." The South asks no relief from its share of this burden. It could not if it so disposed. All it wishes is that the people of the whole country share it with them, which could only be done by separating the two races and by legal enactment of Congress, providing some means and raising the revenue necessary for this great and laudable purpose.

CHAPTER VII.

DOES EDUCATION EDUCATE?

The value of the answer to this query depends largely upon who makes the answer. Of course there are many who will quickly say, " No, that the education of this race is a worthless expenditure of money. They are incapable of receiving or grasping learning of any considerable value." Then there are many more who will answer the query in the negative, in violation, we fear, of judgment, in order to satisfy the feeling of prejudice against the education of the negro, especially when he contributes little or nothing of the pay for the same.

To answer the query truthfully is not an easy task, for the answer certainly cannot be based upon sufficient experience. Therefore, it must be in part speculative. We believe the thoughtful, disposed to honestly and fairly answer the question after careful and diligent investigation, will answer the query in the affirmative.

A generation of experience in the school-room is not sufficient to judge of the intellectual capacities of any people just emerged from a condition of slavish ignorance; but there is underlying this subject, necessary to reach a correct conclusion, an experience which can never be furnished so

long as the two races continue to occupy the
same territory.

It is proposed here to divide the discussion into
two parts:

First, the education of the negro among the
whites under present conditions throughout the
South.

Second, the separate education of this race
colonized after the plan proposed in this work.

Something has already been said of the want
of an inspiring cause in a preceding chapter, yet
in the absence of inspiration, ambition chilled
for want of place and field to display or utilize
their attainments, we find the children of this race
energetic in study, keeping well apace with the
children of the white race, at least until a certain
point is reached, which is usually after the ac-
quirement of a limited knowledge of the three
" R's," reading, riting and rithmetic." This is
the experience and observation of the white Superintendents of the public schools in the different counties having in charge the schools of both
races.   It is the common observation not alone
of superintendents, but of us all.   We might be
permitted to pause here and state, a strong factor
in negro education at the public expense is the
disposition of the parents of this race to compel
their children to attend school, making any sacrifice to this end.   We cannot say as much for
the whites; it is too often the case that white

children are permitted to follow the inclinations of their own mind, which is naturally frolic and play; or for the convenience of parents, are kept at work, when they should be in the school-room, all of which furnishes a strong argument favoring compulsory education.

After the requirement of the three " R's" has been attained, then a perceptible stop is seen, while the white children seem to push forward with greater ease and less exertion, proportionate to the growth of mind, than in the beginning. It is insisted by many that this is because the mind of the negro child has reached the limit of its capacity, while we will endeavor to show in the second division of this chapter, that separate education, after the plan of colonization, will bring out the latent energies of this people, revive in them their ancient glory, dormant during the intervening ages. Still we insist that their education, living among the whites, is by no means a failure, whether the evidence and experience of a generation warrants us in saying what the moral effect of educating the children of this race, or not, this we do know, that the higher institutions of learning for the education of the negro in the South are turning out young men and women by the hundreds, well equipped in mental training for the positions in all the walks of life. One only need attend the Commencement exercises of St. Augustine College

and Shaw University at Raleigh, North Carolina:
Claflin University, South Carolina, and other
colleges in Mississippi, the various higher institutions of learning in Georgia and other parts of
the South, to be convinced that the capacity for
the mental training of this race is far greater
than many are disposed to admit. The minds
of the skeptical, if they could be present at these
Commencement exercises, would be put at rest.
Their apprehensions and fears, that the negro
must be a failure because of inability to learn
and their capacity of intellectual development,
will no longer be entertained, at least will not
have the same ground work for the basis of such
fears and apprehensions.

Now we reach the discussion of separate education, after the plan of colonization.

We would call a man foolish who would in-
vest his fortune and time in anything which
could be after completed, of no value to him.
We would call a man a fool who would work the
best years of his life in acquiring a knowledge of
a thing which could be of no pleasure and certainly of no value, for want of an opportunity to
utilize the same. This reasoning will apply to
the folly of this race, spending their best days
and money in acquiring an education which can
be absolutely of no practical value to them. We
do not mean to say there are no exceptions, and
that education is never useful to the negro, for

certainly a few of them are needed as preachers and teachers of this race while living along with the whites in the same territory. We are not speaking of exceptions. We here mean to speak of the whole race. What need is there of education for the negro under present conditions, further than a limited knowledge of reading, writing. and knowing how to make figures There is no place for them, and they well know it, in the realms of learning along side of his white friends. In the mystic field of scientific exploration, he knows that he is not wanted, whatever may be his attainments, because of the color of his skin. He knows no good can come out of his centering his covetous eye on any of the positions occupied by the great men of this country, just so long, as in such position, he would be the representative of both races. Of what value would the knowledge of the law be to him, when he knows the fondest hopes of his ambition can never be realized in a seat upon the bench of even our inferior Courts.

The physician of this race knows that while it is possible for him to become a member of the Medical Board of the State wherein he lives, yet the disposition to freeze him out will cripple his usefullness and tend to bring him in disrepute even among the people of his own color.

Suppose in some State of this Union we select two locations, equally favored in advantages, with scenery sublime and beautiful, the climate salubrious, in short, equally possessed of all the heart and eye can desire for mental and moral training, and here plant two colleges for the education and training of young men, equip each of these institutions with a President and Faculty of equal merit and ability, and in each make the standard of education the same. At each of these institutions of learning educate annually one hundred young men. To the students of one close all the avenues of greatness, put place and honor, fame and distinction beyond their reach; to the other give them license for entry in the competitive race among men for all positions of honor, fame and greatness, both at home and abroad, as President of this great Republic, as representative of the Court of St. James, as Chief Justice of the United States, the greatest legal tribunal on earth, a seat in the United States Senate, Governors, and all that the ambition of men would hope to attain, would it be difficult to tell in which of these institutions of learning the students would make the most progress. Those denied all the superior advantages given the latter would have the ambition of their souls chilled to the very marrow, college life would be tedious to them, while the latter in the consolation of hope and expectancy, with redoubled energy. would push forward to the goal of success.

Forcibly illustrating this idea, we will give a

little incident. which came under our observation. In the fall of 1896, during the Presidential
campaign, we were driving in a private convey-
ance to an appointment where we were booked
to speak. The driver. a young man and a good
specimen of his race, both physically, mentally
and morally. we had known for years to be a
first-class skillful horseman. It would be difficult to find one who could better manage and
control a team of horses—all the years of his life
he had spent in this business, with no inconsiderable experience upon the turf. I said to him,
calling him by name, " I have confidence in your
ability and skill to manage horses. I expect there
is not much you do not know about this animal.
" Yes," he said, in no spirit of vanity. " I know
something of horse flesh. There is every reason why I should; from my earliest boyhood I
have done nothing else. I like the turf, and am
happiest when driving a horse of speed." But,
said he, " It will never be worth to me more
than the pay of an ordinary laborer, because I
am a negro; the color of my skin makes the training of a life-time worth only the pay of an ordinary laborer beside the white man of equal ability, who will for his services command his own
price."

Well do we know the truth of what this negro
turfman said. This illustration will illustrate all
along the line. No hope of realizing their am-

bition, is it any wonder they stop progress in
schools and elsewhere, after learning only a suffi-
ciency to serve their purpose in the ordinary
affairs of a laboring man.

Colonize this race of people, give them States
of their own, give them State government. In
short, give them all the attendant rights and
privileges belonging to and enjoyed by other people of other States. Then we show you another
view of the picture. Let the children in the
school-room see open a gate-way leading into the
fields of competition, wherein merit and ability
has for its reward, success. Opening up to them
the possibilities of greatness in the particular
sphere of their choice, letting the ambitious eye
of him, who likes the law, see in the distance a
Judgeship. Of him who likes to govern, a Gub-
ernatorial chair. And to those whose tastes run
in the direction of Statesmanship, a place in the
United States Senate or a seat in Congress. Open
the gateway, let these people into the fields of
honest competition and rivalry. Assure them of
the certain realization of the hope of their ambition, whether it be in the way of property getting, as teachers, filling the minor offices or
achieving distinction in occupying the highest
position in the gift of their people, then you open
up the beginning of a new era.

With renewed hope they apply their energies
in a field of attainments heretofore almost un-

known to them. What a difference it must make in the efforts of a man, no matter to what race he belongs, ambitious to achieve distinction, who knows that there is no barrier between him and success save that of honest competition. How blighting it must be to the hopes of him who knows that whatever may be his natural gifts, however great may be his accomplishments, he is handicapped on account of his color, and excluded from participating in the pleasures and enjoyment of those honors, which, under different conditions, is the lot of men of learning and ability.

Colonize these people under favorable conditions upon some spot where climatic and geographical conditions is in keeping with the physical requirements of this race, then let the general Government take auspicious care of them, having a supervising, parental control, with an eye single to their best welfare and success. Then our answer to the query, " Does education educate ? " is with much emphasis, " Yes."

It is hoped the idea contained in this chapter will find lodgment in the minds of those, who in the past have contributed much in the effort to educate the children of this race, and whose hope for their success in the future will cause them to make a careful and faithful examination of this subject, believing that the conclusion reached will be the only successful way of educating the

negro race, is to place them where, when educated, the same field of honor and employment
are open to them, as to the meritorious and successful of other races. This done under the watchful and solicitous eye of the Government, then
education will educate; otherwise, for generations yet to come, there will be much ground for
criticism among those not predisposed in favor
of negro education.

CHAPTER VIII.

THE POLITICAL CONSEQUENCES OF COLONIZATION.

We come now to discuss colonization in its resulting effects upon the politics of the South.

The 13th and 14th Amendment to the Constitution of the United States clothed the negro with all the rights of citizenship, and with unrestricted and unqualified right of ballot. We will refrain from a discussion of the moral right or wrong of this act on the part of the people of this Union, for the purposes of this work we are not called upon to engage in the discussion of that question.

The ignorant negro was well educated by the Republican party in the knowledge of the fact that his freedom and his right of citizenship was its gift; and that in return for it he owed everlasting fealty to this party. No teachers were ever more successful. First, they taught in part the truth, but they seem to have been successful also in teaching that it was the duty of the negro to be everlasting in his fealty. We of the South have long since learned that Ephraim is joined to his idol, and we will let him alone. In latter years the more thoughtful have reached this conclusion, that it is best he should continue joined to his idol, that the political disintegration of the negro as a party is not to be desired.

First, for that so long as he solidly remains a part of the Republican party, and our campaigns are conducted on the color line, it solidifies and unites the white people.

Second, he has learned that the Caucasian will always govern, there is no political preferment for him into whatever party he may go. This, of course, would always make him a floating and purchasable vote, which is not desired in any country. Then, too, he is almost sure, with few exceptions, to unite himself with the less competent to govern, for the reason, we suppose, there lurks in his innermost soul a desire to even up, by inflicting the punishment of bad officials upon the white people who he knows will never permit him to occupy any position of honor or trust or take any part in Government. He also knows that he can stand incompetent and bad officials with far less injurious effect than can his white friends who own the bulk of the property. He is sure always with his vote to jeopardize the progress and prosperity of the section wherein he lives.

It is not our purpose to say (moreover, we disavow such intention), that there are no good Republicans in the South, or that any of these are ever elevated to official positions. We mean only to speak of existing political conditions, which tend to make the solid South; and while temporarily the line may be broken, the same condi-

tions will cause each State temporarily a loss, to
swing back in line.   Again, there is much feeling
manifested between the two races in political
times, even to unwillingness among the masses,
to have the negro vote the Democratic ticket.
The poorer class of white people do not want the
negro to vote with them. Of course this feeling,
the causes which tend to divide the whites from
the blacks in politics in the South might be en-
larged upon.   There is much more that could be
said of the past history of the negro in politics
in the South since the late war.   We might re-
view some of the consequences of his political
acts, in putting upon us in the early days of and
following reconstruction times, bad and wicked
men, whose acts and misdeeds brought us to desperate straights, oftimes to humiliation, shame,
and almost to the very verge of dishonor.   But
we will refrain from further reference; it is not
our purpose to offend any; rather it is our intention, in these pages of this book, to offer facts
proving a condition in support of our argument
for the colonization of this race of people.

All of us know the past and present effect of
these conditions upon our people and section at
Washington. Our treatment at the hands of any
administration is substantially the same.   While
for the past years, the South has been solidly
Democratic, still the great Democratic party of
the United States has regarded it solid as a mat-

ter of necessity, in order to protect its people from negro domination and misrule. This true, we have not received the consideration at the hands of this party which is our due. Likewise a Republican administration is not considerate of the claims and demands or the South, for that it argues, with truth, that the South is a Democratic stronghold. We get nothing in the Electoral College from this section. We therefore have something to gain by bestowing the honorary patronage of this Government, like ambassadorships, consulships and other honorary places upon men of other sections. This is owing to the presence of the negro. The South, great as it is in resources, where the munificent hand of nature has been lavish in her gifts, the climate salubrious—in short, possessed in a large degree of all that goes to make up one of the rarest, richest and most magnificent sections on the globe, populated by a people in intellect, the equal of any, the home in other days of some of the brightest and most conspicuous lights which adorn the pages of our nation's history, is ignored.

It is true either administration may throw out a few crumbs to appease the anger of party leaders in this section, but in the matter of substantial recognition, we have no place, no honors, no gifts, while the hope of a President or Vice-President from this section is only a dream. Politically and otherwise, as we have seen in the pre-

ceeding chapters, this race forms the bone of
contention, the point of divergence between the
sections, north and south of Mason's and Dixon's
line.

To insist that the people of either of these sections desire to keep up this bitterness of feeling
and sectional antagonism is folly. It may be
that for political purposes, orators wave the
bloody shirt, appeal to the passions of their au-
dience in order to insure party success, while the
thoughtful and true of both sections would welcome the obliteration of every vestige of sectional
feeling as one of the richest and rarest gifts from
heaven's storehouse; but alas, so long as they
remain a part of and mixed with the population
of the South. we fear they will continue uninten-
tionally the cause for outbursts of feeling and
bitter contention between the two sections. Colonize the negro and this cause of difference will
be forever removed. Strife between the two sections will end.

The two great parties will divide up the white
people of the South; the great issues of difference between the parties will have as many sup-
porters on the one side as upon the other. Our
local State government will be satisfactory to the
people with either party in power. No longer
will a solid Democratic representation go to
Washington from the different States. The negroes, for some time to come, of course, would

send representatives of only one party. Soon
they would find the necessity of two parties. The
South would then take her proper place in the
sisterhood of States, while the different adminis-
trations will accord to her all that is due.

The fact that a solid vote is given in Congress
for or against any measure by a particular section, furnishes sufficient cause for the united action of representatives hailing from other sections. It is always better for the different sections of this country if the representatives for
each section should divide their vote, and especially would this be true of the South. We have
seen that a combination of circumstances, chief
among them is the negro, has united our people
in the South, sending almost a solid representation to Congress of one party, which, as a rule,
casts a solid vote.

Under colonization this would stop, the solid
South would be broken, the representatives in
Congress would be made up of the two domi-
nant parties, whose vote would be divided according to the necessities of the occasion and as
local interests demand. The negro will become
a student of political economy in his new home.
In politics he will support the party whose policy
best suits the material developments of the section and the progress of his people. A new era
of prosperity would set in throughout the South:
no matter what party at the helm, the ship of

State would be steered into that haven wherein
the material development and prosperity of the
State is best preserved, the happiness and progress of the whole people insured. Offices would
no longer be used as a means of punishing the
oppisition.

In conclusion, the political consequences and
effects alone offer a sufficient argument for the
colonization of this race of people in a place
where they will still be and remain citizens of
the United States, entitled to all the rights and
privileges as such; the general Government
meanwhile having a great care for their well-
being, happiness and success.

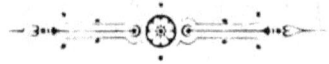

CHAPTER IX.

THE RESULT OF COLONIZATION TO THE SOUTH AS A PART OF THE UNION.

In the truest, fullest and broadest sense the South is in name only a part of the Union. There is a cause for this; many, too many, answering this question without due deliberation, would say, the war of the Rebellion. The pages of history bear record in ancient or modern times of no struggle between men in arms which will compare with that between the boys who wore the blue and the boys who wore the grey.

For fear that some one reading this chapter may misunderstand us, we wish to preface what follows by saying, we are at heart, if we fully understand ourself, truly loyal to this government. We cannot discuss the late war without a sigh intermixed with joy and sorrow; we are truly glad that the slave was made free, glad that our posterity will not have for their inheritance fortunes made in the traffic of human lives, with all the attendant evils common to slavish conditions. We are glad that this Union was preserved unbroken, and we of the South and North have one government, one common country, free to all men. We regret the necessity of the struggle which resulted in the defeat

7

of the boys who wore the grey, whose heroic
struggle amidst great privations has never been
equaled in the world's history. We are glad, that
although defeated, we went down with our face
to the enemy, winning the respect of our foes
and all people, without a blot upon the fair fame
and honor of our glorious Southland. We are
glad that on both sides the war was the occasion
of bringing to the world's view the military genius, eclipsing in greatness and splendor those
who upon the field of battle won fame in any
age.

It is pleasant to contemplate, that after four
years of conflict, amid want and suffering, in
times which tried men's souls, not only did the
men who wore the gray lay down their arms with
respect to the boys in blue, but their heroic efforts,
their almost inhuman struggle against terrible
odds and superior numbers, amid hardships and
trials, won for them as well the great admiration of their generous foes.

At the surrender at Appomattox, the two great
armies parted with good will for each other, but
in contemplation of the hardships of camp life
and bloody battle fields, ripened into real friend-
ship, which has been manifestly and unmistakably shown whenever an occasion has presented,
since those troublesome times. Those who took
part in that memorable struggle sincerely hope
for a reunion not only in name but in fact; those

who would keep afresh the wound and flaunt the
bloody shirt for the war's sake, were those who
knew nothing of the hardships of this great
struggle, who either fought in the great battles
by substitute, or like Job's war horses, sniffed
the smoke of battle from afar. Such knew not
the smell of gun-powder, the roar of the cannon
or the crying whiz of the deadly minie-ball.
Those who answer the causes which make the
South a part of this Union only in name, the
war of the rebellion, are only mistaken. We
must look for another cause.

The fact must not be overlooked, that interested in the great results of the war, there were
far more than those who fought on the field of
battle. The negro was freed, the institution of
slavery abolished, while but few contributed to
aid him in his struggle for existence amid the
new conditions which surrounded him, he became the pet of the many who watched over him
with jealous care, and pounced hawk-like upon
the people of the South for every thing a jealous
mind fancied a wrong done this race, without
understanding the causes or the reasons which
prompted such action. While the soldiers in
blue, and many others who felt like them, wish
these animosities forever buried in a common
grave, yet the editors of newspapers and many
others, without regard to the consequences of
their action, have kept the chasm of separation

apart, with a tendency to deepen and widen. The people of the South, in possession of the frailties common to all men, were naturally incensed. Our soldiers had laid down their arms and returned to their broken homes sincerely desirous of peace and the hope to be let alone in the rebuilding of their lost fortunes, the whole South, with broken hearts over the "lost cause," bowed in honorable submission to the will of the majority and wished complete restoration to the Union. We insisted, yea more, we pleaded to the North and Northern press to be let alone; that our actions were not understood; judgment reached upon the evidence contained in newspapers, who wished cheap notoriety, was erroneous. All, we are sorry to say, was of no avail.

In the halls of Congress, upon the floors of the Senate, this warfare against the South for would-be outrages of the negro, was kept up. Investigations were had, debates followed. Our Senators and Representatives in Congress resenting the interference and defending our people from the slanderous charges, indulged in the use of bitter satire and severe language. They felt keenly the injustice of the interference and the effects of the outrageous slander. Of course we knew, and so did our Senators and Representatives in Congress, that lawlessness and riotous outbreaks would occasionally happen, just as they do in the North and East, sometimes the

court of Judge Lynch called into use and a negro
hanged, just as was recently done in Ohio, and
occasionally done in other Northern and North-
western States; but we thought, and so did our
Senators and Representatives, that it was inquis-
itorial interference for the National Congress to
take upon itself the task of righting these
troubles, of which the State Courts had jurisdic-
tion.

These unpleasant controversies tended to de-
fame our fair country in the eyes of the world,
the influence and usefulness of our Senators and
Representatives in Congress were lessened. The
willing and receptive mind of countless thousands
of the North heard and believed. These circumstances, with the necessity of united action in
the South to protect ourselves from negro domination and misrule, made what is commonly
called a solid South in politics, and as these agencies began to lessen, the mind of the North becoming more at ease and less disposed to excite-
ment, for want of belief of the inflamatory press
publications, men like Senator Hoar, Lodge and
others, for the double purpose of political advan-
tage and humiliating the South, pressed upon us
their inglorious force bill. Such a measure could
only have emanated from the minds not kindly
disposed to the section aimed at, wanting in
statesmanship, in patriotism, and all else but
hatred for the section intended to humiliate.

This latter, had it been successful, would have
been more terrible in its consequences to the
South than all else since the war. That the South
has been kept under a band unwillingly on its
part and denied its true place in the Union and
sisterhood of States, will not be denied by the
dispassionate and thoughtful. That the negro
has f irnished, with no purpose on his part, the
causes of all our troubles, all in search of the
truth will admit; that he will continue to be
the red flag of antagonism between the two sections so long as he remains a part of the population of the South, living among the whites, no
one will doubt.

Thirty-two years have passed since Lee's surrender at Appomattox, and yet it seems we are
no nearer a true solution of the causes of all our
troubles than when we began.

The volcano may for a time cease its eruption,
men may become indifferent to the slumbering
danger so near, still the internal fires burn on,
and at a time when least expected, will belch
forth its destructive lava, destroying all before
it. As the only safety from such danger is to
remove the cause or remove from the cause, the
only permanent peace which can come to the
South and make her in the broadest, truest and
fullest sense a part of the Union, is to remove
the exciting cause of trouble, the negro, by
colonizing this race, putting them to themselves,

separate and apart from the white people. Then,
and not until then, will the South, as a part of
this nation, receive her due, our Senators and
Representatives in Congress be clothed with all
the power and influence incident to their great
offices; then, and not until then will the South,
as a part of this Union, take her place in the
eyes of the world. This done, no longer would
there exist a solid South; the white people would
divide up and stand on the opposite shores of the
great sea of politics. No matter what party in
power, our Senators and Representatives would
be such in the fullest and broadest use of the
term, their influence would be second to none if
merit and ability deserved it; our Southland
would receive that recognition at the hands of
the administration which is her proper due, and
the same as that accorded other sections of equal
power, extent and wealth of resources.

The tide of emigration would set in southward,
with an influx of capital seeking investment,
with assurance to its owner, with no danger of
sudden outbreaks, the result of friction between
the two races to destroy the same. A tidal wave
of prosperity would set in, which would sweep
over our entire Southland. On every side would
be seen prosperity; our mountains and hills
would yield up their store of rich minerals and
gems to the miners, the products of our rich and
fertile valleys would start the spindle and nee-

dles of the factories. Our magnificent forests would be converted into farms, and the timber used to build homes for the settlers, the time would not be distant when the South, one of the garden spots of the earth, rich in resources of every kind, would be converted into one of the richest and most powerful sections of this country. Is all of this desirable? All men will answer " Yes." The nation would answer " Yes," for the strength of the nation is in proportion to the wealth and prosperity of its citizens. The people of the South would answer " Yes," for we wish to see the development of our country, and desire, as loyal citizens, to take our place in the Union of States. All of these things would as surely come with the removal and colonization of the negro as night follows day, while great good would come to this race.

CHAPTER X.

THE RESULT OF COLONIZATION TO THE WHOLE UNION.

"We, the people of the United States, in order to form a more perfect union, establish justice, insure domestic tranquillity, provide for a common defense, promote the general welfare and secure the blessings of liberty, to ourselves and our posterity, do ordain and establish this Constitution."

Our forefathers not only sought under the Constituton to establish a union for our common defense against a foreign foe, but a union of interests for justice, for peace, for the general welfare, liberty, our common good and for the sake of our posterity.

A careful study of this great instrument will show its framers thought that domestic local troubles of any section disturbed the peace and common good of the whole Union. It does not take a Constitutional lawyer to see that it was their purpose to protect and guard against local disturbances in our Union, for the benefit of each part of that Union, as well as for the whole. No man can read the Constitution and fail to see it is made the duty of our Senators and Representatives in Congress, to direct their efforts for the

benefit of the whole Union, in devising a remedy
for the adjustment of all such matters as are
beyond the legislative control of each State or
section of the Union of States.

We of to-day know that the strength of this
nation depends upon the peace, good order and
prosperity of each section. Just as the paralysis
of any one member of the human body affects
the whole body, so does the disorder or derange-
ment of any part of the Union affect the whole
Union. The United States, as a whole, is largely
interested in the race troubles in the South. No
thoughtful man, careful of his words, will say
that order, good will, peace and good feeling obtain between the races in the South. It may be
that the well disposed and wise heads of each
race take no part in these disagreements, on the
contrary, use their influence to avert such, still
the facts remain beyond successful denial, that
these disturbed conditions do exist. How many
instances are almost daily occurring, the papers
of each week contain accounts of several instances where the courts of Judge Lynch have either
been successfully or attempted to be called into
use because of race feeling. The blighting effect
of these differences greatly retards the growth
and prosperity of a large section of this country.
The South is not alone, but the material strength
and progress of the whole nation is affected
thereby. It may not be agreeable to the ears of

many to know that the South is not doing her
duty by one-half in developing her resources, or
in the way of wealth making, and thus contributing her share to the greatness, power and
wealth of the United States; not because of any
indisposition on the part of any of our people;
not because of any mental incapacity, but on account of the presence of the negro race, not much
more than fifty per cent of which are employed,
with as many idle whites, made idle for reasons
elaborately given in another chapter of this
work, which briefly repeated here is the presence
of slavish customs which still obtain, making it
degrading to work with the negro or do the work
the negroes are usually employed to do.   Every
citizen of this Union is affected by the untoward
conditions of the South.

As yet we have seen no solution of the difficulty offered, a continuation of the troubles
which disturb our social fabric, good order and
law are certain to continue under existing conditions.   Emigration and capital in any considerable amount will stay from our borders.   The
best of good will, feeling and brotherly love between the inhabitants of the great Northern and
Southern sections will not be what is desired.
But we have a remedy.   A remedy in which all
should feel an interest, because it concerns all.

Let the people of the United States colonize
the negro and at once a change will set in, so

marked and so great that a stranger visiting our Southern country now and returning again in a few years would hardly know it the same land or the people for the same people.

Does history give us an incident of two nations moving together and living harmoniously upon the same soil? Would the Russians or a large part of their nation move over to England and live happily among the English people? It is likely they would want to return to their native land. Naturally, then, it is not within the pale of reason to expect the white and black man to live in harmonious concord as one great family occupying and peopling the same section.

Every true statesman has at heart the welfare and common good of the whole people. Every true patriot has in his heart love for the whole land of his nativity or nationality. A statesman whose mind is not broad and liberal enough for this, is not a statesman in the broadest and fullest use of the term. A patriot whose heart is not big enough to furnish love for his whole country, is not a patriot, about whom Sir Walter Scott would delight to write.

Our Senators and Representatives in Congress like to be called statesmen without regard for their measurement. Our wise men not in office, who do much to shape the destiny of affairs, wish to be known as statesmen, and to be just, mean to be such. Broad statesmanship, patriotic love, should inspire the great men of this country to undertake the task determind to succeed, in solving the race problem in the South, for the sake of their love of country, but more for the sake of posterity.

It may be that conditions in the South are at present tolerable, but who knows what the future has in store? What man, inspired by the love of his people and the love of his country, is willing to bear with present conditions, to see a great country, inhabited by a great people, stagnant, blocked in the way of progress, peace and happiness; if the troubles can be removed, the difficulty solved, the condition of all made better? Such is the problem of the South confronting the people of this nation.

It is our duty as statesmen, patriots, citizens, as a great people to undertake the solution of this difficulty, for the sake of both races. This is a debt we, the people of the United States owe our own race in the South, a debt we owe to the poor negro, in no way responsible for his presence here, and not to be charged overmuch with blame for the conditions existing in the South.

The whites are better able to take care of themselves. We in the South with white skins ask nothing in the solution of this difficulty, further than the assistance of the brain and thought of the people of this nation, in providing some plan by which a solution, forever settling our race

troubles can be reached, while for the negro we
ask the material and substantial aid.   We of the
South would not ruthlessly turn them aside in
some secluded spot to solve the problem of his
own future fortune. We would not, for the sake
of the memories of the past, we would not forget the happy days of yore, when as slave and
servant he was true to the trust in him reposed,
doing his best for the success of his master's
affairs.

Those of us born in the days of slavery, can
never forget the watchful and almost parental
care of Uncle Tom and Black Mammy.   How
lovingly and tenderly they watched our first
efforts to walk, and with what satisfaction they
listened to the lisping prattle of baby tongues.
We know the jealous pride they had in the children of their owners.   We remember the pleasant hours spent in the cabin listening to the mar-
velous stories of Uncle Tom and Aunt Dinah
about the childhood days of our fathers and
mothers; with what evident pleasure Uncle Tom
would tell that Master in childhood was just the
sprightliest and most active boy in the neighbor-
hood; that Mistress in her girlhood was the like-
liest gal in the county.   While the younger generation of this race may not make the citizen we
desire, may give us from time to time trouble,
yet the man or set of men who will charge, that
we of the South would be forgetful of the past,

that the thoughtful and influential of this section are unkindly disposed to this race, state that about which they know nothing, and which is false, in fact.

You may doubt, " that the sun moves, that the stars do shine, doubt the truth to be a liar," but never doubt the disposition and wish of the Southern people to have material and substantial justice measured out to the negro. In doing them substantial justice, we would have the whole people of this Union to join with us in making his future happy and prosperous. This we believe and insist can be done in colonizing the negro in some happily selected spot, suited in every way to his physical and mental development, letting the people of this nation the while, in every way, contribute substantial and material aid, especially caring for his mental and moral education, and aid him in the formation of his peoples' government in their new home.

The whole Union is interested. The negro race is eight million five hundred thousand strong in this country, and just in proportion as their lot is improved, they are made happier and better, the nation is made stronger. This is true of the white people of the South, as their condition is improved, the resources of this section developed, the power and wealth of this Union increased. It would be criminal in a physician, knowing the disease and cure of a sick patient, not to apply the remedy and restore to health.

One of the strongest members of the body of our Republic is languishing. We know the disease, the cause; we have at hand the certain remedy and sure cure. To insist that anything less than colonization, the separation and removal of the two races from each other, is the prescription of quack doctors, who, owl-like, look wise, and talk much, sell their medicines, draw their pa y, without understanding the disease of their patient.

The proper treatment for disease is, first, to remove the cause and then the cure of the patient. The end of troubles in the South between the races can only be permanently reached by a separation of the two people, and then the cure. The languishing member would then take in new blood, the development of our rich resources would set in, and soon the whole Body Union, affected by the disease of one of its strongest members, will take on new color, new strength, power and influence. This whole Union is interested in the work, and the people of this Union should further it until the results hoped for are accomplished.

CHAPTER XI.

THE TALE OF THE FUTURE WITHOUT COLO-
NIZATION.

In the foregoing pages of this work we have seen something of the feeling between the races existing throughout the Southern States. We have seen how the whites of the South have done their duty in the matter of educating the negro race. We have seen that while he owns but little property and pays less tax, his children have an equal opportunity in the public schools. It is a fact, that in so far as it is possible for the human mind to divest itself of race feeling, he gets equal and substantial justice before the law.

In all places where he comes in contact with the intelligence of the white race, he receives kind consideration and just treatment. In return for all this, the younger generation of this people show nothing but evident ingratitude, no signs of appreciation, and acknowledge therefor no debt of obligation.

The chasm separating the white and black man in the South, instead of closing up, as all good men would desire, is widening and deepening with each coming year. The dislike and hatred the negro bears for the poorer classes of the whites increases. Wherever this race is in

8

the majority, then the true inwardness of real
feeling is seen, their manner is insolent and intolerable.   It is true the younger generation of this
race seem to think their importance, where they
are in the majority, is not felt or understood un-
less he demonstrates in some forceful way his
contempt for the poorer class of whites. No sane
man would ever insist that the whites, under
like conditions, would not be guilty in some degree of similar 'action.   It is, however, a truthful fact, that the negro is largely responsible for
the conditions which exist throughout the South.
Patience is ceasing to be a virtue, with a generous people, who for thirty odd years have done
so much to better the condition of the freed man,
to see in the generation which has come on since
the abolition of slavery, so ungrateful, and show
so little appreciation for the favors done.   '' Patience ceases to be a virtue'' with the whites of
the South, who for thirty-odd years have helped
the negro in trouble, sheltered him in stress of
weather, administered to his wants in sickness;
in short, done what they could in every way to
improve and better him; to have in return for it
only a disposition to humiliate his benefactors,
to aid at the ballot box with his vote in placing
in power to govern, not one of his own color;
for that would be impossible, but in many instances those whose policy in every way tends to
check the material growth and prosperity of our
Southern country.

Common talk among young negroes of the concessions they have wrung from the white people, and in the coming day, when with superior numbers they will whip the whites into submission to their will, which is often overheard, tends to make lines hard for this people.

It is not wisdom to blind ourselves to real conditions, better far it is to prepare for the storm and seek harbor before we are in the midst of its destroying fury. " In times of peace, let us prepare for war." It would be well for the wise men of our country, in this day and generation, to drop the scales from their blinded eyes and see the conditions existing between the two races in the South as they are, to draw aside the veil of futurity, look down the vista of time, and see the result of race feeling in the South. They know, if they are willing to see, hear and be convinced, that we are resting upon a burning volcano, which while at present gives no signs of eruption, is gathering within the forces which sooner or later will belch forth with all of its fearful consequences, ruinous in its effect of one of the best sections of country on the globe. In the meantime, our commerce and trade will languish, our agricultural interests gradually lessen until our farmers become their only consumers, our mineral and other resources undeveloped. In short, instead of becoming one of the greatest sections of this great Union, which might reasonably be expected, on account of the salubriousness of the climate, the fertility of the soil and the great magnitude of our undeveloped wealth and resources, we will drag along doing as we have done, ekeing out a most miserable existence.

Do the signs of the times point to good results for the future in continued habitation, side by side with each other of the two races in the South ? For answer to the query, we point the reader to the preceding pages, wherein the author has been careful to state truthfully the facts fairly and impartially as they concern each race. If we have been unjust we disavow any intention of such.

Do the signs of the times in continued habitation of Southern soil by the two races point to bad results? Our answer is, " Yes, to both races, just as certain as night follows day, just as sure as the crow of the cock or the song of the early bird are the signs of coming morn." Then it is certain that race feeling is becoming more intensified and dangerous in its character as the years go by. "There are none so blind as those who will not see, none so deaf as those who will not hear." Men of the South, men of the North, men of all parts of this glorious country, have you eyes and see not ? have you ears and hear not the truth ? Conditions of race feeling in the South as they are, will you longer be hypnotized into a state of happy ignorance, of the widening and deepening chasm separating the two races?

While the South has done her duty towards the freedman and his children, is willing still as a just people to continue to open the doors of our storehouse to the mental, moral and physical necessities of this race, ungrateful as they are; yet the time is coming when the bridge will no longer bear its intolerable burden; our people will tire of the practices of this race.

It is natural, and even commendable in the negro to celebrate each returning anniversary of his freedom, permissible for him to take part in the Fourth of July celebrations. he is a citizen of this country, and has a right to celebrate her glorious past. Such action on his part is hopeful evidence of a proper appreciation of the great and glorious country of which he is a part, of the pride he takes in the future of his race, and all thoughtful men will commend him for it.   But when this race of people so far oversteps the bounds of propriety as to celebrate the anniversary of Lee's surrender of the Army of the South, they are adding insult to injury. fuel to the burning fire, race feeling, and shows unmistakable evidence of the growing dislike between the masses of these two races.   We believe it will be a surprise to many to know this practice has been inaugurated, to what extent we are not as yet prepared to say. We do know that in Henderson, North Carolina, and perhaps in other places in this year, 1897, it was done. This would not offend, because of the results of the war and freedom of the slaves, for the South would not have him back in his previous condition of servitude; but the celebration and rejoicing at our defeat in the most manly and heroic contest between brave soldiers the world has ever seen; celebrated, too, in our very midst, on Southern soil, and in the very presence of those who participated in that great struggle, is naturally calculated to offend. Thoughtful men of each race cannot control this feeling, or bridge over this chasm of separation, try as they may. The signs are increasing, and point as unmistakably toward trouble in the South, if existing conditions continue in those sections where this race has become powerful and great, by reason of its superior numbers, as the gray dawn of the morning and the red light in the east are evident signs of the coming sun.

While the white race in the South have done much for the blacks, we at the same time owe something to ourselves, and in due time, when the season is ripe for it, they will resort to such measures as will certainly insure safety and security to our posterity, though it be at great loss and sacrifice. Wise men of this country, Christian women, whose influence is great in high places, be no longer deluded, awaken to the truth, see the situation in its true light, and by common action, with one united purpose now while we can, avert the awful consequences which await the people of the South, without regard to color or race. Let us do now while we can that which will insure peace and happiness to both races, wealth and prosperity to one of the most magnificent sections of our common country. The longer we postpone this work, the greater will be the undertaking. To neglect it would be criminal. Posterity in future years will cry out against us for our wilful failure in removing the cause which we well knew would bring upon our descendants troubles, the breadth and extent of which we cannot measure.

The pages of the future historian will be marred with strife between the races, riotous outbreaks, civil war, Southern soil again drenched in blood, not in a conflict of arms with other sections, but among and between the inhabitants of our own fair Southland.

CHAPTER XII.

THE TALE OF THE FUTURE WITH COLONIZATION.

We do not believe the millenium is at hand, or
that the world is so Christianized, men have
ceased to think or do evil. We do, however, be-
long to that class who know that there is yet
much good, much of the milk of human kindness in the hearts of men. When the great majority have come to take an account of stock and
examine the real feeling of their hearts, jeal-
ousies and sectional strife will give place to better sentiments, good will and happiness for all
mankind. We are confident that all people within the pale of this Union wish for the general
peace, happiness and prosperity of every section
thereof. In this belief we invite the attention
of the people of the United States to a solution
of the race problem in the South.

Of the necessity of action in this direction, we
will not speak in this chapter. The reader is re-
ferred to the preceeding pages for facts and argument to sustain this need. We propose herein,
with a draft upon the imagination, to paint a picture of the future after colonization. It will not
be so much the work of imagination either, for
we believe, in the foregoing chapters, sufficient
proof has been given to furnish substantial and

material coloring matter for the picture, while
the good will and united action of the whole
people, through our Congress, would furnish the
strong frame of protection to the picture we will
present.

Separate the two races, cause the negro to
move to the land set apart for him, to plant his
own vine and fig tree, and the whites living upon
the same soil to move out, make room for his
uninterrupted course of self-government; have
the people of this Union contribute substantial
and material aid in his mental, moral and physical development; send among them missionaries
who have their success at heart, to educate them
in the art of government; in short, in every way
supply the deficiency in their own material resources until they have had full and sufficient
time to become self supporting, not in a bare
possible subsistence, but in peaceful, happy and
prosperous success; educated morally, mentally,
and trained physically—all this done with the
kind and parental good will—we have then gathered together the material for our picture.   With
paint pot and brush in hand, let the work begin; let the world look on the rough material
gathered for the work of the artist, examine the
base of the structure, the land given them for
their future home, the inhabitants as they now
are, then abide its time for a generation, while
the work of the builder and painter is going on.

In the meanwhile, over among the whites another picture is in progress, in sole occupation of their own territory, where they live in exclusion of the other race, they are painting the picture of their future.

Let us now pause. For a generation the negro has been colonized; the white and black man have lived separate and apart, occupying separate and distinct territory. The world's attention is invited to an examination of the negro nation in America, settled in the Southern part of the United States. With amazement and surprise they see a happy, peaceful and prosperous people, the unmistakable evidence of which is seen all around, broad acres well cultivated, yielding abundant crops to the husbandmen, on every side neat and happy homes, with inmates in neat attire, with well-filled corn cribs and smoke house, stock-houses with horses, cattle and hogs in plenty are found everywhere, well attended schools with competent teachers dotting every hillside, the steam whistle and hum of machinery is heard in every village, factories giving employment to thousands in every town, at each county seat strong jails and ornamental court houses furnish the unmistakable proof that law and order is enforced; church spires everywhere pointing heavenward, where each Sabbath day the people are taught the ways of the meek and lowly Jesus, the value of moral

life and of the life to come. At the capital cities
magnificent State buildings and great officers,
chosen because of their peculiar moral and intellectual fitness to govern their people for the greatest good; a healthy public treasury; the public
debt and taxation in keeping with the requirements of a happy, prosperous and progressive
people; their State bonds selling above par in all
the markets of the world; contentment is seen
everywhere; the haunts of vice few; the virtue
of their women comparing favorably with that
of other women; divorces seldom; race pride
evident; while at the same time they show great
good will for other people, often giving expres-
sions of grateful acknowledgement to the white
people of the United States and their Southern
white neighbors for making colonization possible, and for the substantial and material aid
given them in their nations new home, with
great promise everywhere of a still better future,
looking to the revival of the ancient glory of
their African ancentors.

Nor have the whites been idle; the Southern
country occupied by them has become the envy
of a critical world. In the place of strife, the
result of race feeling, we see peace, good will and
obedience to law. The idle thousands kept out
of employment at the time when the two races
occupied the same soil, because of certain customs which obtain, are at work; plenty and com-

fortable homes have taken the place of want and
miserable huts; the population has been largely
increased by millions of successful farmers and
thousands of skilled artisans and factory employ-
ees; the faces of all are marked with the evidence of a happy and prosperous people learned
in the art of money making; no longer the care-
worn faces of yore. Our villages have grown
into towns, our towns into great and populous
cities. Our magnificent forests have been converted into fertile farms. In a generation the
population of the South has doubled, not made
up of that class who threaten the peace and good
order of society, but of a healthy wealth-making
class, given to good morals and strict obedience
to law. General stagnation and sloth have given
place to the bustle and activity of busy life.
Capitalists, no longer afraid of racial disturbances, threatening the security of their fortunes,
have found profitable investment, investing millions in developing the resources of our Southern country. The South, always agricultural, is
now a manufacturing people as well. In politics,
the people are divided between the two great
parties; no longer a solid delegation of one political faith is sent to represent the section at the
nation's Capital. The pendulum of success
swings from one to the other great parties; the
South has taken her place of power and influence in the councils of this nation, the wave of

prosperity has swept over the entire Southland. Tourists returning from their travels through the South among both races tell of a people prosperous and happy, and of a beautiful land, which floweth with milk and honey.

Such is the tale of the future in the South after colonization. Without it stagnation of business everywhere, farms grown up, fences decaying; want and discontentment mark the faces of the unhappy people; race conflicts disturbs the peace and order of society; the march of progress turned backward; that great expanse of country, which should be the garden spot of the world, if not a barren waste, at least the Rip Van Winkle section of the United States.

Statesmen, patriots, noble men and Christian women of this great country, we appeal to you and ask if the picture is not worthy of your careful consideration.

CHAPTER XIII.

WHERE SHALL WE COLONIZE THE NEGRO?

In selecting the location for the colonization of the negroes of the United States two things should be considered:

First, his presence here against his will; the use made of his brawn and muscle.

Second, a climate and section suited to his mental, moral, physical and constitutional development.

In considering the first division of this subject, we are reminded that he was brought to our shores against his will and in chains, the willing consent of his mind and heart played no part in this work. No one will deny that his transportation, from the wilds of Africa into conditions of slavery in the United States has resulted in great and incalculable good to this people, and may be the means and agencies employed in the unknown future of civilizing his entire race at home in Africa. The fact that he was at the time of his coming, an unwilling visitor, gives him a claim at least with hope based upon expectation of just and fair treatment. They ruthlessly torn from home and friends, brought amidst strangers, who became his masters and had the benefit of his service as slaves for gener-

ations, certainly would expect kind and just consideration in his freedom from the hands of those
directly responsible for his present condition.
Moreover, his brawn and muscle in the days of
yore, with axe in hand, felled the trees in our
mighty forests, cleared the sites for our cities
and towns, and made the plantations for our
fleecy white cotton. What the South was before
the war between the States was largely the result
of his labors, great crops of lint and other materi-
als which supplied the markets of our new world
were the products of his work, the value of his
own body and person was added to the value of
our wealth, while the product of his toil was the
gain of the white man. If our people were powerful and influential, he made them so. Nor to
be just, should we be unmindful of the fact, that
he has done his share in the development of our
resources since the war; and in whatever of progress we have made in rebuilding our broken fortunes since that terrible conflict, he has done
much, notwithstanding the barrier, the result of
race feeling and conditions existing, of which we
have heretofore spoken, to the general prosperity
of our country. We should not be unmindful of
what he has done in the past, and the part he
has had in the slow progress of the South in latter days.

Again, the fidelity of the negro at all times to
the interest of his owners while in slavery, and

especially the unparalled example of his faithful
watch of Southern homes, our mothers and sisters, wives and daughters, while the gray were
battling with the blue to perpetuate his slavery,
should at least claim our kind and thoughtful
consideration.

The love of humanity should play its role in
the selection of the spot suited to the needs of
the black man.   The good people of the United
States would be unwilling to put him beyond the
pale of touch and easy communication; undoubtedly their pupose and wish would be to better
his condition.   To do this it would be necessary
to have him in reach of assistance at some point
where the Government could have an immediate
view of his situation, necessities and the progress
he is making, where the results of colonization
could be watched, not by a few, but by many,
and where quick remedies could be applied in
the weak spots wherein the plan of colonization
needed quickest assistance.   Where our people
could be by example his teachers and in easy
reach of missionaries, who, for the love of humanity and the welfare of this race, would help
him on to success.   These reasons, of course,
play a strong part in the selection of territory for
this people.

We now approach the second point to be considered in this chapter, the climatic and geographical situation with regard to their mental,

moral, physical and constitutional development.
The negro is a plant of hot-house requirements;
he came from the sunny tropics of Africa; he is
not accustomed to a cold climate, nor will his
physical composition admit of exposure to ex-
cessive cold; he becomes an easy prey to the ravages of pulmonary diseases, common to cold countries.   In a large majority of instances, where
they go from the Southern States to the Northern cities, they soon become victims to consump-
tion.

The beginning of the slave trade was in the
New England States. This was soon abandoned,
for the reason just given. It was found unprofit-
able, because he could not stand the severe cold
of New England. Gradually the commerce turned
to the South.   It was found the tropical suns of
the Southern States was better suited to his physical and constitutional needs, and more like the
hot climate of Africa, from whence he had been
brought..   Of course, then, any idea of a region
where severe cold and winter are common, would
be suicidal and out of the question.   Nor would
any place beyond the pale of United States, as
some have suggested, be considered for a moment, because it would be eminently unfair, unjust and bad treatment, like which the people of
the United States could not and would not be
guilty of.   Under our Constitution, by our own
act, we made him a citizen of the United States.

He came here not of his own will, brought here through the agency of our people, it behooves us then from every possible moral standpoint to give him an equal chance in the race of life, besides that any other course could not be taken without amending our Constitution, which our people, in that particular would never permit.

Since the foot of this race was first planted on our soil, he has lived upon every part of the United States, during which actual experience has shown that he thrives better on Southern soil than elsewhere, the climate is nearer like that of his native home, than we have elsewhere within our borders.

Nor would it be right, if colonization is possible, to colonize in some new and unbroken region, like Arizona or New Mexico, which has been suggested by some.   Then, without doubt, the place of the United States best suited to the requirements of this people, is in that belt nearest the Gulf of Mexico and in the Mississippi Valley, found in the three States of Mississippi, Alabama and Louisiana: and if these three be found insufficient, then Arkansas might be added. There are two controlling reasons for selecting Alabama, Mississippi and Louisiana.   First, our Southern climate is all that is desired in these States for the health and constitutional needs of the black man. In the second place, already there are more of this race of people living there than we find in any other three States of the Union, with a largely increasing and growing tendency during the past decade, to emigrate and settle here from other sections; the natural increase of the negro population in these States, augmented by this gradual but constant stream from other sections, will in the very near future be so great that the white population will be lost, overwhelmed in this growing sea of black humanity. Nearly one-third of the negro population of the United States live in the three States above named, while about seven-eights of the whole negro population live here and in other Southern States, in close proximity to these three.

Again, there are more negroes in these three Southern States than there are whites.

The census of 1890 shows a total colored population in Alabama, Mississippi and Louisiana of 2,002,240, while the total white population is 1,936,280, a difference of 65,960. The total number of the negroes living in the United States in 1890 was 7,638,360. Calculating on the same ratio of increase from 1880 to 1890 for the years from 1890 to 1897, we have now living in the United States 8,385,845, of which about 2,202,464 live in the three States of Alabama, Mississippi and Louisiana, less than one-third and considerable more than one-fourth of the entire negro population.

We find, including the proper ratio of increase

of both races, from 1890 to 1897, there are whites
and blacks together, 4,332,864 living in these
three States, with room a plenty for four or five
times as many more; having the white population to move out, we have here territory sufficient to contain the entire negro population of
the United States, not only of to-day but for a
century to come.   In view of the fact that near
one-third of this people already live in these
States, it would be less difficult to get others to
go with their people living there.   The author is
confident that when the matter of place is carefully considered, after recounting our obligations
to this race, his physical inability to withstand
colder sections, the injustice of sending him upon
untried and unbroken soil, the fact that experience has shown that he is happy, healthy and
contented in the sunny cotton belt of the Gulf
section, the conclusion will be reached with irre-
sistible force, that duty says Alabama, Mississippi
and Louisiana is the favored spot.   Here, as before said, his race are already in the majority,
yet living well, traveling the road of life and success at a commendable pace, with institutions of
learning for this race as good as the best, where
he is in as easy touch of the white people of this
country as it is possible to place him; this section
of all others is the favored one to be the future
home of the negro nation living in the United
States.

CHAPTER XIV.

WOULD THE WHITES EMIGRATE FROM THE SECTION SELECTED FOR THE NEGROES ?

Of course our white friends living in Alabama, Mississippi and Louisiana when first put to them, would give a very positive and decided "No" for their answer to the question, would they emigrate from their States, sell our their farms and homes, and bid adieu forever to the land that gave them birth. Nor is it a question which could be promptly answered, it is of such momentous proportion that its answer would require much deliberation and careful study. This done, when they have come to examine the matter in the light of wisdom, looking as well as can be into futurity, for the sake of posterity, then, doubtless, would be the beginning of a reconsideration of the first answer. Slow would be the process of reasoning for the solution of the problem. The answer to the question put to them is a serious one, the magnitude and greatness of which cannot be easily measured.

We are well aware there are many serious and perplexing questions to be answered by the people now occupying this territory, some of which would stir the uttermost depths of the great sea of sorrow, the hallowed memories of the past,

rebelling against the sacrifice of the heart. The
abandonment of scenes of childhood and the
happy traditions of our ancestors, the land of glorious achievements of our forefathers and patriotic dead. The birth place of Southern statesmen and the home of Jefferson Davis, whose
achievements, though condemned by others,
form pages of glorious and adorned history in
the minds of all Southern folk. Who can read
the reminiscences of plantation life in ante bel-
lum days in the South, no matter in what section of the United States he may reside and not
find an opportunity in his own mind and heart
to say these were indeed good times, beautiful
country and a happy people? The memories of
all this to be forgotten, the land of these hallowed associations given up, makes the answer
all the more difficult, as difficult as it is, yes,
though a thousand times more difficult. Southern soil is now and has been for all time indige-
nous to a noble race of people, brave, heroic, glorious in past achievements, patriots indeed, who
for the love of country and posterity will in conclusion reach an answer in keeping with their
past glory, self-sacrifice and patriotism, an answer which will be for the good of the whole
Union, of the whites of the South, and especially
good for the negro race. Their answer would undoubtedly be "Yes" to the question, the problem
of which so vitally concerns our posterity and
the future of our once glorious Southland.

They see through the mist of years the frightful consequences of intercommunion and life upon the same soil of the white and black races. While conditions may be tolerable, and hardly tolerable now, yet the passage of time which gradually brings us to the distant future, is also gradually unfolding a tale which would mar the pages of the future historian. Especially is this true in that section wherein this race is largely in the majority, and who as time gradually comes and goes will more and more assert their power. Another thought here we will mention, which will assist the people of this section in giving a favorable answer, is that the white race in these States will not increase except from natural causes, while the tendency of negro emigration is already to these parts, which in future will rapidly increase, for the reason that, they like race power; and as intelligence with them increases in future, more and more will the disposition to emigrate thither grow upon them.

No one expects that our people in this section will at once sell their homes, either to individuals or the general government, abandon their possessions and move away to make room for the negro race. This work must be one of slow growth, but come it certainly will; if it is a sacrifice, which we seriously doubt, will for the sake of posterity, certainly be made. Conditions may be tolerable to-day, but every true man and parent wishes to better his affairs to-morrow, and for the sake of his children struggle to leave them an inheritance, morally, mentally and materially better than was his; an all-wise Providence has made the parent love in all nature, strong and self-sacrificing, the ties of parental obligation is the incentive which moves men and women to great deeds for the sake of their offspring. The same parent love, common to all nature, planted in the breast of creation by an all-wise Creator and akin to God-love, will inspire the white people of the South, for the sake of their children and posterity, for the sake of unborn generations, through whose veins will flow their own blood for all time, will solve the problem which disturbs the present and threatens the future even into annihilation of the weaker race by moving out, surrendering their home and the land of their nativity, to make room for the abode of the black man, ending race conflict, restore peace, order and obedience to law, where disturbances and dangerous outbreaks threatening the good order and well-being of society, now exist, and in so doing, build for themselves a monument which for self-sacrifice for the good of their country and the love of their own race, will be the pride and glory of posterity.

CHAPTER XV.

CONCLUSION.

We have seen in the foregoing pages of this book the animosities and race feeling existing between the white and black races in the Southern States.

We have seen the causes which have led to this deep-rooted dislike for each other. How that certain Northern papers are pleased to fan the already burning fires, for none other than the selfish purpose of enlarging their circulation and increasing their bank account, causing the impassable gulf to deepen, widen and lengthen beyond the possible hope of ever bringing its shores in touch one with the other.

How that certain persons in the beginning helped to plant the seed of discord, yes, even hatred, by talking of amalgamation between the noble race of people that live in the Southern States and the negroes, their former slaves. We have seen that these causes are increasing as the years go by, and as the old ex-slave gradually passes away, their influence lost upon the younger generation, the negro race becomes more intolerable to the whites; while the latter, forgetting plantation memories, the tales and traditions of the happy past, as the older heads die out, have less of regard and kindly feeling for this people.

Time, the great absorbent, fails to wipe out the unpleasant memories of the past, for the reason that, the repetition of still more offensive action opens the wound afresh, fanning the fires of hatred and dislike between the poorer class of the white race and the negro race, until the utter annihilation or dispersion of the weaker is imminent in the distant future.

Passing on we find the plan of colonizing the negro a practicable one.

That this race, if given an opportunity under the auspices of the general Government, with the good will of the people of this Union and the assurance that he would be helped onward in the race of life, would embrace the plan of colonization, move out from among the whites of the South and into the region given them for the future abode of his people.

We believe that we have shown that this race has the capacity of self-government; that thrown upon their own resources would develop their latent and hidden energies, and instead of being dependent, would become independent, self-reliant, more disposed to better their conditions, and in every way capable of an existence separate and apart from their white friends.

We have certainly demonstrated that his presence among the white people of the South is a

barrier to the onward march of prosperity. With
no intention to hinder and delay, he does check
Southern progress, and while thousands of his
own race are idle because of the existence of
certain untoward conditions, common to the
South, the immediate results of the careless and
indulgent habits of slave masters in the days of
slavery, and whose careless and extravagant
habits makes it possible for the employed of this
race to maintain thousands of their people in
idleness, his presence, because of certain inexorable laws of society, makes thousands of idle
whites oftimes without the simplest necessaries
of life in a land of plenty, who, but for the presence of the negro, are willing and would be indus-
triously employed, gathering about them comfortable homes with plenty, at the same time adding to the nation's store of strength and wealth.
We have seen his removal would solve this problem of Southern stagnation, causing the unemployed and idle of both races willingly and gladly,
we believe, to become industrious workers instead of idlers. We have shown how willingly,
and we will here add gladly, the white people of
the South self imposed the great task and
weighty burden of educating the children of this
propertyless race; how that while they own no
property and pay no taxes, the Southern whites
with generous heart and open hand have divided
the school fund equally among the children of
both races, in proportion to numbers.

We have shown the injustice for the Southern whites to bear this burden alone for the education of a race once their property and made free without compensation, not by themselves, which fact would present a different case, but by the people of the United States.

We have shown that the negro should be the care of the whole people of this Union, if the idea obtaining among the many is true, that this race is to become God's chosen means and instrument for the civilization of the negro nation in barbaric Africa, then the better and more perfect his education, sooner and more certain will this work be accomplished, which should be the desire of all good and Christian people, not confined alone to the South, but to this entire country.

We have also seen that the education of this race among the whites for reasons fully given does not educate; that colonized, the possibilities of greatness opened to him in all the avenues of life, that in the world he has an equal chance in the field of competition for honorary seats in any and all the positions and high places open to people in other countries, would furnish an inspiration for thorough and efficient education.

The political results to the Southern States have been discussed, proving that the solid South in politics is the direct result of the negro's presence at the polls. His colonization and separation, we have shown, would result in the division of the whites of the South, taking their place in equal numbers, in all probability, in the ranks of each of the old political parties. The administration at Washington, looking with favor upon our sunny South, no matter which party in power, that we would receive our due recognition and take our honorary position in the sisterhood of States and in the eyes of all the world, being known, as in truth, we really are, a great part of this Union, in the enjoyment of all the rights and privileges accorded to other sections of our country, while our great men and statesmen, according to merit and ability would be given those places at home and abroad, which rightly belongs, to what will become under colonization, one of the strongest and wealthiest sections of this Republic.

The good result coming to both races after the plan of colonization proposed has been mentioned, evil practices, the sin of adultery between the races would be forgotten, while no one can calculate the good which would follow in the wake of the idle employed, which, we think, would certainly be conspicuous among the good results to be attained.   We have seen the value of colonization to the Union, that whenever any section of a great country is bettered, the whole country just in that proportion is made stronger, more capable of resisting unfriendly foes from without, the nation wealthier, the people happier. The tale of the future, with and without colonization, tells us on the one hand of the slumbering volcanic dangers which abide, almost hidden to the many, but are sure to come, like a landslide in the distant future, freighted with awful consequences to both races, and destructive to the peace and prosperity of one of the best sections of this Union, while with colonization all over a great and extensive section of country, the future will unfold a story of happy people, both white and black men, patriotic and loyal, wealthy and prosperous, a Union cemented with unbreakable bands, where sectional strife, like which we have witnessed during the past generation, between North and South, will be no more.

We have seen that in climate, in geographical situation with regard to the physical and moral necessities of the black man and the convenience of the Government, in easy communication and assistance, we have at home in our own borders a region of country in every way suited for the colonization and future home of this race, and believe we have assigned reasons strong and sufficient to induce the whites already living in the same to move away and make room for the negro.

Should the negro be colonized? ''Truth, virtue and happiness are the Heaven intended heritage of man; their ultimate triumph over the broad surface of the moral world is the promise of the Bible. God has laid His universe under contribution to promote the happiness of men, and where untoward conditions and circumstances have withheld from him facilities allowed him by heaven, we are called upon by the great Father of all to correct the evils, if we have it in our power to do so, by supplying the deficiency. It is what the happy to the unhappy owe."

We believe separation a part of the plan of the Creator; while for a century the negro in America has learned much in the school house of white training, of which his people in native Africa would never have known anything; that the hand of Providence may have and we believe did have something to do with the erection of the school rooms in which his people have been trained for a century, that a great and wise purpose was in view in this work; that the still greater possibilities of civilizing and christianizing this benighted race within the confines of barbaric Africa, yet we insist the time is ripe, under the Divine plan, for the parting of the waves, the separation of the two races in the United States.

Those who believe that the hand of Providence directed the enslavement of the negro here; that at the appointed time, subsequently caused his freedom, for the great work of futu-

rity in civilizing his brother in Africa, must see
he is making haste slowly. We have seen the
reasons of this slow haste, that among the white
people higher education is of no value to this
race; while on the other hand, we have seen that
this race, if educated in the hope of full fruition
of reward for his services in acquiring great
knowledge, he would, like other people with an
opportunity given, apply all of his energies to
this end, which blessing would come with colonization.

We believe it is the plan of the great Creator
that separate races and nationalities should have
a separate existence, in order for the complete
fulfillment and teaching of the Divine law,
"Thou shall love thy neighbor as thyself." To
whom was this command given? By turning to
the xix Chapter, 18th verse of Leviticus, we see
it was the command of God spoken to Moses, the
lawgiver and God's own appointed leader of the
Israelites as the rule of action between neighbors, the members of the tribe of Israel. Would
any one contend for a moment that this command of God to Moses, a part of the code of laws
for the government of the Israelites, would have
been given as the rule to be observed between
the Israelites and the Egyptians while in bon-
dage in Egypt? Will theologians contend that
this command was given to Moses as the rule of
action between Israelites and other nations? We

think not. Repeating here the whole of the 18th verse, " Thou shalt not avenge nor bear any grudge against the children of thy people, but thou shalt love thou neighbor as thyself; I am the Lord." it will be seen that the command was given to Moses for the people of Israel, no other were contemplated in its meaning. It is clear that at the time the command was given to the lawgiver, for the guidance of God's chosen people, none other were intended than the Israelites alone; moreover, we believe it would be in violation of this great commandment, which our Lord Jesus Christ says is like unto the first, and upon which hangs all the law and the prophets, in violation of natural laws, to expect people of different blood, different race, different nationality and differing in color of skin, to love each other as they love themselves. Do the French love their German neighbors as they love their own nation ? Are not the English jealous of all people ? Do the Irish love their English neighbors ? Are the people of the United States much in love with the Spanish people ? What is true of nations is true of individuals. Obedient to nature's laws and natural instincts, an Englishman could and would not hold a Chinese neighbor in the same esteem and have for him the same kindly feeling he would for one of his own nationality or kindred race. Do the citizens of the United States love an Indian neighbor, even if

10

domesticated, as he would one of his own people ? Do we not see in our Northern cities the Italian and the Chinese, more of the German and French having their separate quarters, gathering the people of their nationality together, then will it be contended that they love their neighbors of different nationality and blood as they do their own people? We might extend this argument further in the realms of nature, and prove that animal kind do not live and associate with each other of the same genus but differing in specie. This is likewise true of bird and fishes. We do not mean to compare the human family with animal nature, except in so far as their natural tendencies admit of comparison. We all know that the human family, robbed of our intelligence and education, would instinctively follow our natural inclinations just as wild nature in animal kind does. No one would insist that, according to natural laws, there would ever be any admixtures of races. We conclude, then, when Moses was given the commandment by God, it was for his own peculiar chosen people, the Israelites. To say, " That thou shalt love thy neighbor as thyself," was meant by the great Creator between neighbors of different nationalities would be to violate all natural laws, which, as well as the great Second Commandment, are God's creation.

To insist; then, as some have, that the white

and colored people of the South should literally
observe between the races this great Commandment of God, given to Moses for the guidance of
the Israelites, would be in violation of all natural laws and the Divine law of God.   We wish
to be understood.   We do not mean to say, that
there is not good will and good feeling between
many of the two races in the South, yea more,
many of us, very many of both races, would
have still more if we could control, of brotherly
love between these two people, but mean to say
and do say, the two races of the South do not,
and obedient to nature's laws, cannot and never
will love each other as they love the people of
their own race.   Therefore we insist, for the complete fulfillment of the Divine law, colonization
is in order.

In conclusion, we ask all well-meaning, thoughtful people of the United States to consider well
the pages of this work. If, after careful thought,
you reach the conclusion that the chasm between
the races is deepening and widening; that race
feeling of hatred and dislike for each is increasing and growing; if you find in your conclusion
that colonization would result in removing the
barrier to Southern prosperity, greatness and
progress; that the burden of educating the blacks
is too great for the Southern people alone, who
for a generation past have done their full duty;
that the education of the negro among the whites

is a failure; if you believe that the claim that
education of this people colonized would be successful, is sustained by the argument used; if
you believe that the solid South would be broken
and great good come to each of the races living
upon separate territory; that the South, as a
part of the Union, would take her proper place
in the sisterhood of States and in the eyes of the
world; if you believe the whole Union would be
strengthened, lines of sectional difference oblit-
erated, the people and the whole country bettered thereby; if you are of opinion that the tale
of the future without colonization would be one
of woe to our Southland and to the two races,
as the signs of the times unmistakably point;
that the future gives promise of nothing less
than ruin and desolation to one of the fairest
lands upon which the foot of man ever trod;
war and bloodshed between the races, resulting
in the utter annihilation of the weaker, which
could be averted by separating these people in no
way kindred to each other; that with colonization the mantle of peace would be thrown over
the land made sacred with the memories of the
past, drenched in the blood of our Revolutionary
forefathers, where mixed with mother earth,
sleep the ashes of those who contributed much
to this nation's glorious past on the field of battle, in the halls of Congress and upon the bench;
that the future, with colonization, would pre-

sent two races living in neighboring States, happy, prosperous and progressive in the arts and sciences, keeping apace with the march of civilization, each contributing to the nation's greatness in peace and in war, and adding much to her storehouses of wealth and power, if you believe that with colonization, higher and better educaton will come and again abide with this exslave race, whose ancestry in the remote ages of antiquity were in civilization and enlightenment, in advance of all mankind; if you believe it a part of the plan of Almighty God to Christianize all men, that the negro in the United States could be made an instrument in the hands of Providence in civilizing and Christianizing his people in native Africa; that these instruments in the hands of God would infuse this once great people with new blood, new hope, revive in them the memories of their glorious past, and inspire them with energy and activity, intelligence and greatness to resist the unjust encroachments of other nations of the earth, then in God's name, we appeal to you for the sake of humanity, for the love you bear your own white brother, through whose veins courses the same blood, and who sprung from the same proud ancestry, for the sake of this fallen race once great, with us you put your shoulder to the wheel and push the glorious work onward.

Statesmen and patriots, jurists and lawmak-

ers, novelist and poet, indeed the services of all
men we engage in this great work, and ask with
relentless determination, you push on in your
efforts until the mark of success is reached, the
bell of your target is rung, the bull's eye is hit
with glorious achievement.   When the glory of
your success shall be heard in poetry and song
throughout the ages of futurity by the two happy
races occupying the sublimely beautiful land of
the South, whose music by the breezes shall be
borne over the bosom of the great ocean to the
shores of Africa, and there caught up by the inhabitants of a once famous and glorious country,
who with their posterity in the myriad of ages
yet to come, send heavenward your praises to the
throne of a great and merciful God, who will reward the posterity of your loins for the good
work of their forefathers. Noble men and Christian women of this fair land of our sisterhood of
States, to whose shores Liberty seated on a throne
beckons the oppressed people of earth, a great
work lies spread out before you.   If, as statesmen, you wish to ameliorate the condition of all
men, your attention is invited to the unhappy
posterity of the ex-slaves in the South and the
idle whites, who, on account of conditions beyond their control, are made miserable and sub-
jects of want in a land of plenty and promise;
if, as patriots, you can appropriate the language
of Sir Walter Scott, " Breathes there a man with

soul so dead, who never to himself has said, this
is my own, my native land," and wish to see all
the inhabitants thereof happy, peaceful and prosperous, then we point to the Southland and ask
you to look upon a people occupying one of the
fairest portions of earth, hating each other,
whose animosities threaten the peace and prosperity of our land.

As novelists, we ask you to tell in story the
condition of the South, and with the genius of
imagination, give to the people of our country
the picture of a people again restored to the glo-
ries of their forefathers in the remote ages of antiquity; tell of our fair land occupied by different nations in separate territory, the home of the
happy and the free, where order and law are observed and the courts of Judge Lynch unknown.
As poets, tell us not of the heroic struggle of our
forefathers for independence, the triumph of
their arms against the British foe, already this
occupies the first place on the roll of fame; not
of camp life and victories in Mexico, for this,
too, adorns a brilliant page in our history; tell
us not of a Union made strong with the growth
of a century, composed of indestructible parts,
cemented with the best blood of our land; nor
of the marvellous growth and strength of our
nation and country, the admiration and envy of
a civilized world; tell us not of the broad and
fertile plains, of the sublime scenery and grand-

eur of the Rocky Mountains and the great West,
but go with us to other fields, with pastures
green, come to the land of flowers in our sunny
South, a land of promise without progress;
where two races, unlike to each other, un-
happily live. Come here and for us sing of the
future, with colonization of this beautiful land
of the vine and the rose, of broad lakes and
sounds, majestic and graceful rivers, mountains
grand, with scenery sublime, of valleys beautiful, green hills and flowery dales, of minerals
rich and rare, grand forests and fertile farms,
sing a new song, whose melodies will sink deep
in the hearts of our Southern people, and whose
music and rhythm assures us that the fire of genius in your poetic soul is being kindled, in flames
of love, to burn out existing conditions and blaze
a new Elysium in Dixie's land.

Ministers of God, we wish to interest you.
·Preach to your people this problem, and how
it can be solved. Say to them, it is a common
duty to better all mankind. If you are fully persuaded, then petition the great King of earth to
hasten the consummation of this great work, the
result of which will be to thoroughly educate the
negro, to prepare him for the great work of taking Christ crucified to that once great and now
benighted people. Christian women, in you we
hope to find our best workers. Oh, for another
Harriet Beecher Stowe to write of the need of

separation and colonization as she wrote of the causes which led to the abolition of slavery. Are there not others such who would espouse this cause, throwing in it the fervor of their souls and being, as none but a woman can? Point out to the people of our country the great necessities of separating the two races, and of the awful consequences awaiting us in the future if this wise course is not taken in this day, when the problem is easy of solution.

Women of this country, noble women of the North, South, East and West, we invite you to take part in the solution of this grave problem. It is a duty, a Christian duty you owe to mankind, a duty you owe to the negro, in no way responsible for his presence here. It is a duty you owe to the white people of the South, of the same race, same nationality, same flesh and blood, of which you justly boast. We ask you to speak with your husbands and sons, engage their grave and earnest attention, and with you join in a common effort to solve this perplexing problem. Noble women of the South, descendants of a proud ancestry, wives of patriotic husbands, and mothers of brave sons, we appeal to you to awaken from your lethargy, and for the sake of your descendants, we ask you to study this greatest of all problems which confronts the Southern people, now easy of solution, but which if left alone, will in future years disturb the peace and order of our fair land we love so well, and threatens the very existence of your posterity.

Negroes of the South, foremost men of your race, to you we appeal and ask attention to the greatest problem which concerns your people in this country.

We believe we have conclusively shown that the race feeling in the Southern States is growing, the chasm dividing the two races deepening and widening, that education of your people among the whites is a failure; that separate education, after the plan herein proposed, giving to your nation all the rights and privileges in your new States and homes accorded to other citizens of the United States, would be a great success. Then we point you to the glorious achievements of your African ancestors in ages past. We invite you to examine your nation's early history. In it you should find hope and encouragement. Study the comparison of the conditions attending your race in Africa of to-day and in the ages past; for the sake of your now oppressed nation, the prey of all people in benighted Africa, resolve that with God's help, you will now begin the work with unrelenting application, which shall have for its results, the freedom, civilization and moral emancipation of more than one hundred million of your unfortunate brethren. Especially do we ask your consideration of the impending dangers which threaten your people and the whites as well, in continued existence and habitation together on the same soil.

Colored men of thought and brains, you cannot fail to see that the future of your race under continued present conditions is not full of promise; you know well among the whites there is no room at the top of the ladder for the genius of your race, no matter what your attainments, your moral virtues, your intellectual ability, you can never hope to aspire to high places. We ask you to go with the mind and the imagination to the sunny land of Alabama, Mississippi and Louisiana, and with prophetic vision look into the future of your people here colonized under the auspices of our Government, with the whole people of the United States back of you, contributing to your moral and physical necessities, making thorough and complete your education, with a right of representation in Congress, given to the other members of the sisterhood of States; aiding you in the establishment of a perfect State government, and see a progressive, prosperous and happy people, unknown to strife and bitterness of feeling, now common in the South to the races, then resolve what your people once were in the remote and distant past, you can and will again be, and in the hands of God, become instruments for the redemption of your brethren in your native land. These blessings can only come to you colonized.

Lastly, to those who read these pages, let us say, in the depths of our innermost soul and in the secret recesses of our heart, there exists nothing but good will and kindly feeling for the man of black skin and a sincere desire to better his condition. This feeling, and the hope of doing good to one of the fairest and most promising portions of earth, and the noble race of people, sprung from a noble ancestry, has prompted the author to write these pages. If, in these imperfect suggestions, anything has been said to cause our people to study the race problem, leading to the perfection of a plan of separating the two races in the South, bringing peace, happiness and prosperity, wealth and power in the place of hatred and dislike, sloth and backward strides in the march of power and greatness to our sunny South, then the author will be consoled in the thought that his labor has not been in vain.

For several years Mr. E. S. Simmons, the author of this work, has been totally blind.

APPENDIX.

It may be the white people living in the States wherein it is proposed to colonize the negro would welcome a solution of the problem in separation and colonization of this race, but would be unwilling to abandon their possessions, leave their homes, to which they are bound by a thousand ties of memory and association—the homes and possessions of their forefathers and parents, hallowed by the memory of childhood and made dear as their birthplace: home and first playground of their own little children. While we are irresistibly forced to the conclusion that the three States, Alabama, Mississippi and Louisiana, are in every way better suited for colonizing the negro race than any other section, and that the whites in these States should move out and make way for their uninterrupted course of self-government and separate existence; yet if their unwillingness to give up their homes and possessions forms an insurmountable barrier to the plan of colonization as proposed in the pages of this work, then, in answer to this objection, we say in these States there is territory sufficient to block out three new States for the negro race large enough to contain this people for a century to come. If this be not enough, we have, near by, in Arkansas and Texas, room a plenty. The whites can gather themselves together in those portions of these States nearest the Gulf coast, their beautiful cities by the sea, and near the mouth of the great Mississippi river. Retain the names of the States as they now are, thus making six States of the three. This would enable the white people living in these States still to remain, for the most part, near the scenes of their childhood. The object to be attained is colonization of the negro race in separate States. The white and black man will not—yea, cannot—live in peace and harmony together. Separation of the two races and the colonization of the negro must and surely will come. It is for us to say whether we will now solve the problem in an easy and amicable way, or will we, like cravens, leave the task to our posterity; if so, the consequences of our actions, will be awful to contemplate.